BADGES   and DISTINCTIVE INSIGNIA

of

The Kingdom of SAUDI ARABIA

CAPTAIN DAVID V. OLSON, QMC

ISBN: 0-9609690-0-4

U.S.A.
1981

U.S.-Saudi Arabian Joint Commission on Economic Cooperation

ACKNOWLEDGEMENTS

The badges and distinctive insignia illustrated in this booklet are from my own personal collection. It is hoped that this book will assist researcher, historians, and collectors in the pursuit of their work and/or hobby.

This book was made possible due to the technical assistance of Major Roy J.C. Thompson, Canadian Armed Forces,and Mr. Harry Pugh, Editor of <u>Chute & Dagger News-letter</u>, for encouragement to seek out the elusive airborne insignia/badge variations. Additionally, special thanks to my former Fort Knox neighbor, CPT Fred Stuhrke, Signal Corps, for introducing me to the art of military insignia collecting in 1975. But especially to MSG(Ret) Gilbert McFadden an ASMIC member whom I have admired and respected over the years. Additionally, CWO(Ret) Richard W. Smith(Smitty) of Erin, Tennessee for his kindness, encouragement and advice. But, most of all to my family for their encouragement and patience over the past years.

I would be most happy to correspond with serious collectors in the further pursuit of information to make this booklet and future booklets more complete. Please see Chapter XV for mailing address.

Regards,

D. V. Olson

FUTURE BOOKLETS

Vol. 2 - ROYAL SAUDI AIR FORCE: BADGES AND DISTINCTIVE INSIGN
OF THE KINGDOM OF SAUDI ARABIA.

Vol. 3 - SAUDI ARABIAN NATIONAL GUARD: BADGES AND DISTINCTIVE
INSIGNIA OF THE KINGDOM OF SAUDI ARABIA.

Vol. 4 - ROYAL SAUDI NAVAL FORCES: BADGES AND DISTINCTIVE
INSIGNIA OF THE KINGDOM OF SAUDI ARABIA.

Vol. 5 - PARA-MILITARY FORCES: BADGES AND DISTINCTIVE INSIGNI
OF THE KINGDOM OF SAUDI ARABIA.

Vol. 6 - FRONTIER FORCES: BADGES AND DISTINCTIVE INSIGNIA OF
THE KINGDOM OF SAUDI ARABIA.

Vol. 7 - SAUDI ARABIAN MILITARY SERVICE RIBBONS AND MEDALS.

Vol. 8 - SAUDI ARABIAN CIVILIAN AND MILITARY DECORATIONS AND
MEDALS.

Vol. 9 - SAUDI ARABIAN OFFICIAL SEALS AND LOGOS FOR THE
KINGDOM OF SAUDI ARABIA.

Vol. 10- INDEX OF VOLUME 1 THRU 9.

H.M. King Khalid Ibn Abdul-Aziz Ãl-Saud

Iraq
Sinai
Jordan
Tabuk
Al Ba
F
Egypt
Buraydah
Al Qasim
Medina
Jidda
Taif
Mecca
Kingd
Sudan
Abha
Khamis
Red Sea
Yemen A
Republi
Ethiopia

Iran
ait
Arabian Gulf
h'ab
Jubail
Qatif
Dammam
Bahrain
Dhahran
Al Khobar
Qatar
Dubai
Gulf of Oman
dh
Al Hasa
Al Kharj
United Arab
Emirates
Masqat
Saudi Arabia
Sultanate of
Oman
Empty Quarter
Peoples Democratic
Arabian Sea
Republic of Yemen
den

CONTENTS

INTRODUCTION AND BACKGROUND
CHAPTER I

This pictorial booklet is designed primarily for that
)up of people who indulge in the hobby or business of col-
:ting, trading, buying, selling, manufacturing and designing
military badges & insignia. Another group which will find
.s booklet very helpful are those whose interest is limited
an area study---in this case Saudi Arabia in particular and
: Middle East in general. Then there are those who can see
it through the medium of military insignia/badge collecting
it the world is, in essence, quite small with a host of
:tors interacting which influence the manner, dress, insignia,
ges and espirit within the armed forces of a particular
intry.

Distinctive insignia has tended to evolve as organizations
developed, modified, expanded, redivided, remodified and
xpanded. The Kingdom of Saudi Arabia is no exception to
s basic premise. Advice and assistance from allies, friends,
internal personnel and activities has seen remarkable
gress in this area of insignia development as well as devel-
ment of structured functional military organizations.

The effort of collecting a medium such as badges and
ignia in the Middle East and Saudi Arabia in particular,
a labor of love, but was also cause for frustration, dis-
ointment and temporary discouragement. A redeeming point,
ever, were the friendships and acquaintances developed
ing the quest for the various pieces of illusive Saudi
bian Military Badges and Insignia.

I am sure it was difficult for my local contacts to
erstand, at least at that time, why anyone would want
ious pieces of current insignia, let alone old and
olete insignia of a bygone era. I can only say, "These
ious pieces of metal and cloth represent the Saudi's
itary History--a documentation of the armed forces pro-
ssive development." I hope I am able to clearly show
s development in a pictorial manner which will be a credit
the Kingdom of Saudi Arabia and the Saudi Arabian Land
ces.

The following pages in Chapter I show my own personal
lection of Saudi Arabian Army Insignia and Badges.

AIRBORNE BADGES & INSIGNIA

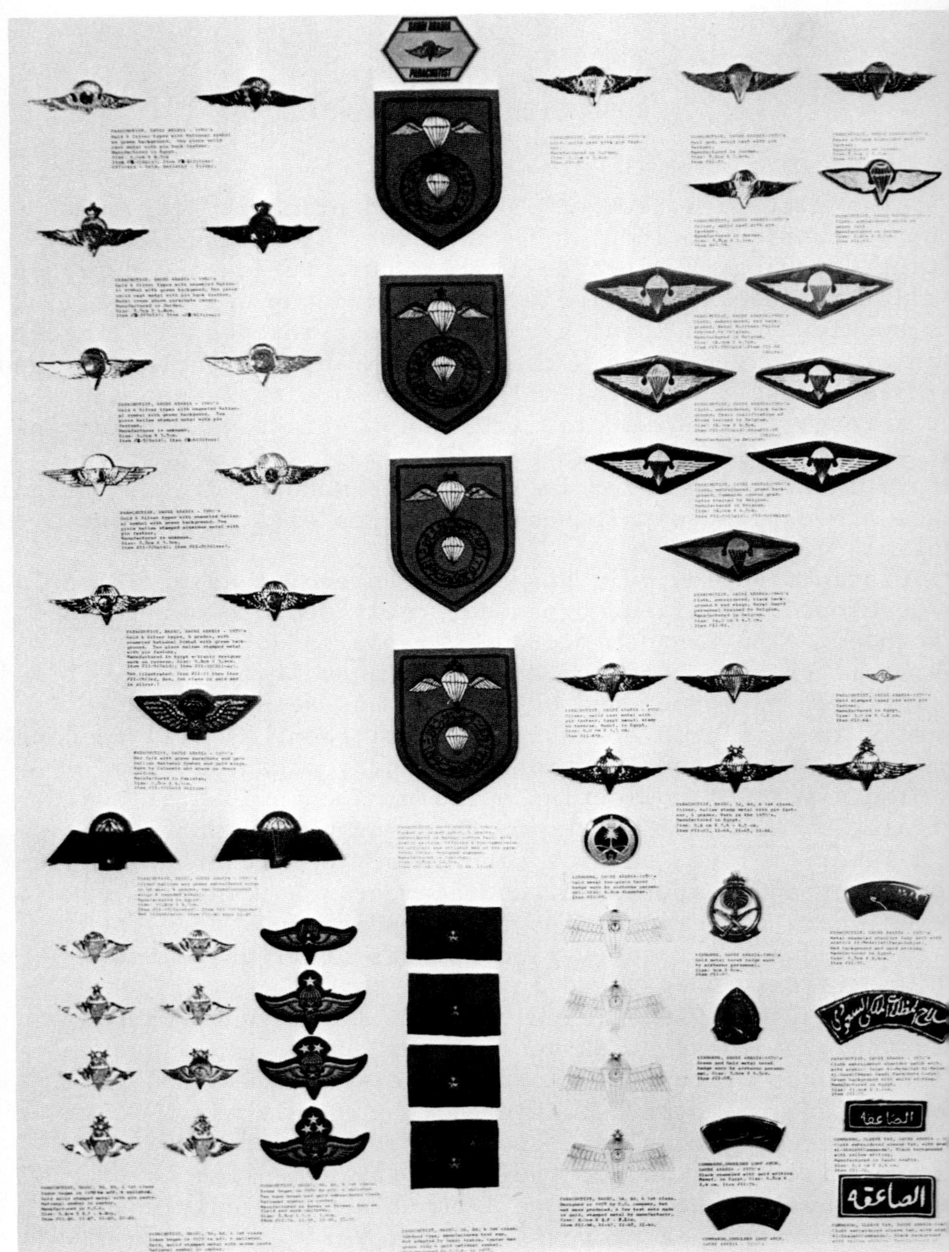

AUTHOR'S COLLECTION OF CHAPTER II
ITEMS

SAUDI ARABIAN CAP, HAT & BERET BADGES

AUTHOR'S COLLECTION OF CHAPTER III
ITEMS

ENLISTED CHEVRONS

&

WARRANT OFFICER RANK BADGES

OFFICER RANK BADGES & GORGETS

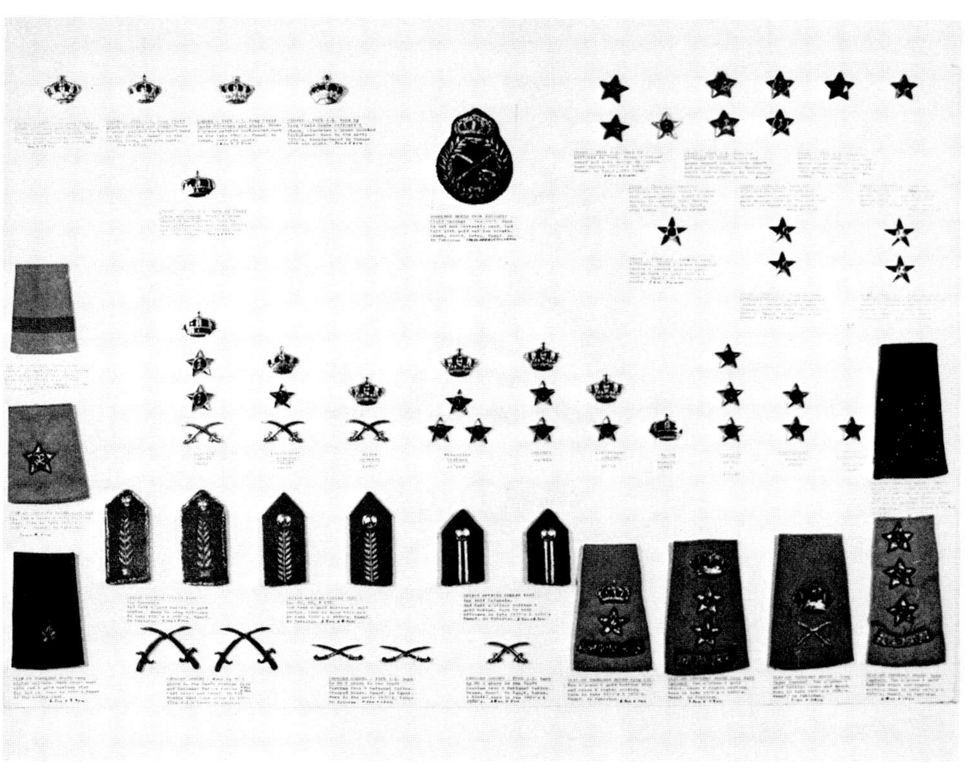

AUTHOR'S COLLECTION OF CHAPTER V
And VI ITEMS

BRANCH OF SERVICE BADGES

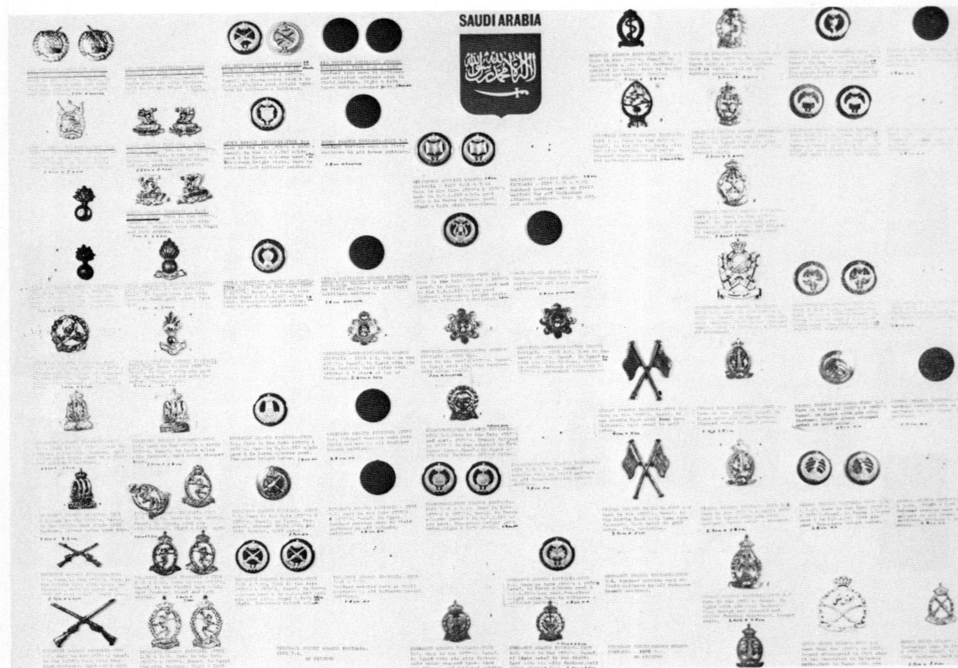

AUTHOR'S COLLECTION OF CHAPTER VII
ITEMS

SHOULDER ARCHES & PATCHES

AUTHOR'S COLLECTION OF CHAPTER VIII
ITEMS

U.S. GOVERNMENT ORGANIZATIONS IN SAUDI ARABIA

AUTHOR'S COLLECTION OF CHAPTER XI
ITEMS

U.S. GOVERNMENT ORGANIZATIONS IN SAUDI ARABIA

AUTHOR'S COLLECTION OF CHAPTER XI
ITEMS

AIRBORNE BADGES AND INSIGNIA
CHAPTER II

Saudi Arabian Airborne Insignia/Badges were first issued in the late 1950's and early 1960's. These first wings made no distinction between levels of expertise or the number of jumps completed. These first or early versions had a crown attached to the top of the parachute canopy. This crown was similar in design to that shown on the following pages of Chapter II. The gold wings were worn by officers and silver wings by enlisted soldiers. Egyptian and Jordanian manufacturers influenced these early wing designs, as Saudi Arabia does not manufacture any of its own airborne wings or insignia.

The number of wing variations in evidence is considerable since Saudi Arabia has had airborne forces for less than 30 years. However, each variation is uniquely distinctive and the manufacturing process has shown increasing quality over the years. Until the late 1970's a total of 10 different basic airborne wing variations were being worn by airborne soldiers and ex-airborne qualified soldiers.

The current airborne wings, in gold only, with four(4) grades, are well made and of superior quality and design. These wings are worn by both officers and enlisted. The following countries have made contributions to Saudi Airborne wing design & manufacturing: Egypt, Jordan, Pakistan, Belgium, Korea, Taiwan, and the United States of America.

A variety of metals and cloth have been used to make this fascinating array of airborne wings.

The following pages are examples of the various airborne wing types, styles, and variations currently identified as being currently or previously used by Saudi Arabian Airborne Forces.

PARACHUTIST, SAUDI ARABIA - 1950's
Gold metal with national symbol on green
background. One piece solid cast metal
with pin back fastener. Worn by officer.
Manufactured in Egypt for Saudi Arabia.
Size: 9.0 cm X 2.7 cm.
Item #II-1.

PARACHUTIST, SAUDI ARABIA - 1950's
Silver metal with national symbol on green
background. One piece solid cast metal with
pin back fastener. Worn by enlisted.
Manufactured in Egypt for Saudi Arabia.
Size: 9.0 cm X 2.7 cm.
Item #II-2.

PARACHUTIST, SAUDI ARABIA - 1960's
Gold metal with enameled national symbol
on green background. Two piece hollow stamp-
ed metal with pin fastener. Worn by officer.
Manufactured in the Middle East for Saudi
Arabia.
Size: 9.0 cm X 3.5 cm.
Item #II-5.

PARACHUTIST, SAUDI ARABIA - 1960's
Silver metal with enameled national symbol
on green background. Two piece hollow stamp-
ed metal with pin fastener. Worn by enlisted
Manufactured in the Middle East for Saudi
Arabia.
Size: 9.0 cm X 3.5 cm.
Item #II-6

PARACHUTIST, SAUDI ARABIA - 1960's
Gold metal with enameled national symbol
with green background. Two-piece solid
cast metal with pin back fastener. Royal
crown above parachute canopy. Worn by
officer. Manufactured in Jordan for Saudi
Arabia. Size: 8.8 cm X 4.2 cm.
Item #II-3.

PARACHUTIST, SAUDI ARABIA - 1960's
Silver metal with enameled national symbol
on green background. Two piece solid cast
metal with pin fastener. Royal crown above
parachute canopy. Worn by enlisted personnel.
Manufactured in Jordan for Saudi Arabia.
Size: 8.8 cm X 4.2 cm.
Item #II-4.

PARACHUTIST, SAUDI ARABIA - 1960's
Gold metal with enameled national symbol on
green background. Two piece solid stamped
aluminium metal with pin fastener.
Manufactured in the Middle East. Worn by
officer.
Size:8.8 cm X 3.3 cm.
Item #II-7.

PARACHUTIST, SAUDI ARABIA -1960's
Silver metal with enameled national symbol
on green background. Two piece solid stamp-
ed aluminium metal with pin fastener.
Manufactured in the Middle East. Worn by
enlisted.
Size:8.8 cm X 3.3 cm.
Item #II-8.

PARACHUTIST, BASIC, SAUDI ARABIA - 1970's
Gold metal with enameled national symbol on
green background. Two piece hollow stamped
metal with pin fastener. Four(4) grades in
gold worn by officers. Manufactured in Egypt
with arabic designers mark on reverse.
Size: 9.2 cm X 3.4 cm.
Item #II-9 thru II-12.

PARACHUTIST, BASIC, SAUDI ARABIA - 1970's
Silver metal with enameled national symbol on
green background. Two piece hollow stamped
metal with pin fastener. Four(4) grades in
silver worn by enlisted. Manufactured in
Egypt with arabic designer's mark on reverse.
Size: 9.2 cm X 3.4 cm.
Item #II-13 thru II-16.

PARACHUTIST, BASIC, SAUDI ARABIA -1970's
Red felt with green parachute and gold
bullion national symbol with gold bullion
wings. Worn by Colonels and above on
dress uniform. Four(4) grades.Manufact-
ured in Pakistan for Saudi Arabia.
Size: 9.8 cm X 4.1 cm. Item #II-17. Not
shown: Item #II-17a, 17b, 17c. 3d, 2d,
& 1st class.

PARACHUTIST, BASIC, SAUDI ARABIA -1970's
Silver bullion and green embroidered
wings on OD wool, with pointed wings.
Four(4) grades. Worn by officer & Enlisted on OD uniform. Manufactured in
Egypt for Saudi Arabia. Size: 10.2 cm X
4.7 cm. Item #II-18.

PARACHUTIST, BASIC, SAUDI ARABIA - 1970's
Silver bullion and green embroidered
wings on OD wool, with rounded wings.
Four(4) grades. Worn by officer & enlisted on OD uniform. Manufactured in Egypt
for Saudi Arabia. Size: 10.2 cm X 4.7 cm.
Item #II-19. Not shown #II-20 thru II-25.
(3rd, 2nd, & 1st Class-pointed & rounded)

PARACHUTIST, BASIC, SAUDI ARABIA -1979/80
Gold solid stamped metal with pin posts.
National symbol in center. Four(4) grades
worn by officers and enlisted. Manufactured in U.S.A. & Korea. Size: 6.2 cm X
2.7 cm. Item #II-26(USA); Item #II-30
(Korea)-screw posts.

PARACHUTIST, 3d Class, Saudi Arabia-1980
Gold solid stamped metal with pin posts.
National symbol in center. Worn by officers and enlisted. Manufactured in U.S.A
and Korea. Size: 6.2 cm X 3.5 cm.
Item #II-27(USA); Item #II-31(Korea-with
screw posts).

PARACHUTIST, 2nd Class, SAUDI ARABIA-1980
Gold solid stamped metal with pin posts.
National symbol in center. Worn by officers and enlisted. Manufactured in U.S.A
and Korea. Size: 6.2 cm X 3.5 cm. Item
#II-28(USA); Item #II-32(Korea-with
screw posts).

PARACHUTIST, 3rd Class, SAUDI ARABIA-1980
Gold solid stamped metal with pin posts.
National symbol in center. Worn by officers and enlisted. Manufactured in U.S.A
and Korea. Size: 6.2 cm X 4.2 cm.
Item #II-29(USA); Item #II-33(Korea-with
screw posts).

PARACHUTIST, BASIC, SAUDI ARABIA - 1980
Two tone brown and gold embroidered cloth.
National symbol in center. Worn by off-
icers and enlisted on field & work uni-
forms. Manufactured in Korea or Taiwan.
Size: 8.5 cm X 3.9 cm.
Item #II-34.

PARACHUTIST, 3rd Class, SAUDI ARABIA-1980
Two tone brown and gold embroidered cloth.
National symbol in center. Worn by off-
icers and enlisted on field & work uni-
forms. Manufactured in Korea or Taiwan.
Size: 8.5 cm X 5.2 cm.
Item #II-35.

PARACHUTIST, 2nd Class,SAUDI ARABIA-1980
Two tone brown and gold embroidered cloth
National symbol in center. Worn by off-
icers and enlisted on field & work uni-
forms. Manufactured in Korea or Taiwan.
Size: 8.5 cm X 5.2 cm.
Item #II-36.

PARACHUTIST, 1st Class, SAUDI ARABIA-1980
Two tone brown and gold embroidered cloth
National symbol in center. Worn by off-
icers and enlisted on field & work uni-
forms. Manufactured in Korea or Taiwan.
Size: 8.5 cm X 5.9 cm.
Item #II-37.
Note: Item #II-34 has merrowed edge.

PARACHUTIST, BASIC, SAUDI ARABIA - 1980
Manufacturers test run of subdued type,
cloth embroidered, black on OG twill.
Center has green ring with gold national
symbol. NOT ADOPTED BY SAUDI ARABIA.
Manufactured in U.S.A. Size:6.0 cm X 2.6
cm.
Item #II-38.

PARACHUTIST, 3d Class, SAUDI ARABIA-1980
Manufacturers test run of subdued type,
cloth embroidered, black on OG twill.
Center has green ring with gold national
symbol. NOT ADOPTED BY SAUDI ARABIA.
Manufactured in U.S.A.
Size: 6.0 cm X 3.4 cm.
Item # II-39.

PARACHUTIST, 2nd Class, SAUDI ARABIA-1980
Manufacturers test run of subdued type,
cloth embroidered, black on OG twill.
Center has green ring with gold national
symbol. NOT ADOPTED BY SAUDI ARABIA.
Manufactured in U.S.A.
Size: 6.0 cm X 3.4 cm.
Item # II-40.

PARACHUTIST, 1st Class, SAUDI ARABIA-1980
Manufacturers test run of subdued type,
cloth embroidered, black on OG twill.
Center has green ring with gold national
symbol. NOT ADOPTED BY SAUDI ARABIA.
Note: Rings of other colors denote branch
Manufactured in U.S.A. Size: 6.0cm X 4.0
cm. Item # II-41.

PARACHUTIST, Patch, SAUDI ARABIA - 1960's
Pocket or Jacket patch, Basic, embroidered on maroon cotton twill with arabic
writing:Officers & Non-commissioned
officers & enlisted men of the paratroop
corps. Designer unknown. Manufactured in
Pakistan. Size: 9.8 cm X 12.8 cm.
Item #II-42.

PARACHUTIST, Patch, SAUDI ARABIA - 1960's
Pocket or Jacket patch, 3rd Class, embroidered on maroon cotton twill with
arabic writing:Officers & Non-commissioned officers & enlisted men of the paratroop corps. Designer unknown. Manufactured in Pakistan. Size: 9.8 cm X
12.8 cm. Item #II-43.

PARACHUTIST, Patch, SAUDI ARABIA- 1960's
Pocket or Jacket patch, 2nd Class, embroidered on maroon cotton twill with
arabic writing:Officers & Non-commissioned officers & enlisted men of the paratroop corps. Designer unknown. Manufactured in Pakistan. Size: 9.8 cm X 12.8cm.
Item #II-44.

PARACHUTIST, Patch, SAUDI ARABIA - 1960's
Pocket or Jacket patch, 1st Class, embroidered on maroon cotton twill with
arabic writing:Officers & Non-commissioned officers & enlisted men of the paratroop corps. Designer unknown. Manufactured in Pakistan. Size: 9.8 cm X 12.8 cm.
Item #II-45.

PARACHUTIST, BASIC, SAUDI ARABIA - 1978
U.S. manufacturers test design in gold
stamped metal. A few test sets made.
NOT ADOPTED BY SAUDI ARABIA.
Size: 6.0 cm X 2.7 cm.
Item #II-46.

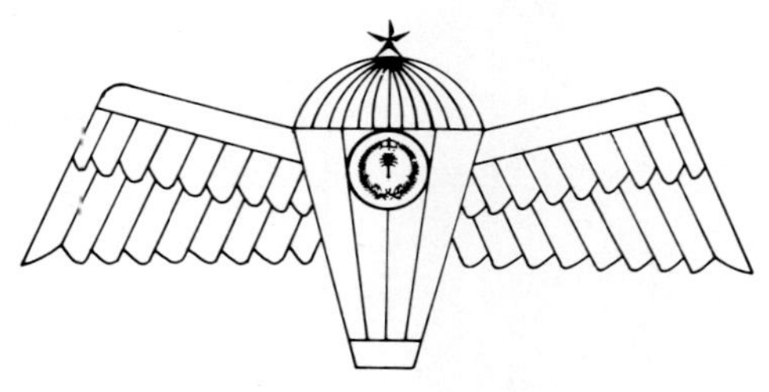

PARACHUTIST, 3rd Class, SAUDI ARABIA-1978
U.S. manufacturers test design in gold
stamped metal. A few test sets made.
NOT ADOPTED BY SAUDI ARABIA.
Size: 6.0 cm X 3.1 cm.
Item # II-47.

PARACHUTIST, 2nd Class, SAUDI ARABIA-1978
U.S. manufacturers test design in gold
stamped metal. A few test sets made.
NOT ADOPTED BY SAUDI ARABIA.
Size: 6.0 cm X 3.1 cm.
Item #II-48.

PARACHUTIST, 1st Class, SAUDI ARABIA-1978
U.S. manufacturers test design in gold
stamped metal. A few sample test sets
made. NOT ADOPTED BY SAUDI ARABIA.
Size: 6.0 cm X 3.5 cm.
Item #II-49.

PARACHUTIST, BASIC, SAUDI ARABIA - 1970's
Gold, bright, solid cast with pin fastener.
worn by Saudis trained in Jordan.
Manufactured in Jordan.
Size: 9.0 cm X 3.2 cm.
Item #II-50.

PARACHUTIST, BASIC, SAUDI ARABIA - 1970's
Gold, dull, solid cast with pin fastener.
Worn by Saudi officers trained in Jordan.
Manufactured in Jordan.
Size: 8.9 cm X 3.2 cm.
 Item #II-51.

PARACHUTIST, BASIC, SAUDI ARABIA - 1970's
Brass metal with black highlighting and pin
fastener. Worn by Saudi officers trained in
Jordan.
Manufactured in Jordan.
Size: 8.9 cm X 3.1 cm.
Item #II-52.

PARACHUTIST, BASIC, SAUDI ARABIA - 1970's
Cloth, embroidered with white on green felt.
Worn by Saudi officers trained in Jordan.
Manufactured in Jordan.
Size: 9.2 cm X 3.7 cm.
Item #II-53.

PARACHUTIST, BASIC, SAUDI ARABIA - 1970's
Silver, solid cast with pin fastener. Worn
by Saudi enlisted personnel trained in Jordan
Manufactured in Jordan.
Size: 8.8 cm X 3.1 cm.
Item #II-54.

PARACHUTIST, SAUDI ARABIA - 1960's
Cloth, embroidered, gold wings with red back-
ground and yellow border stitching. Worn by
Royal Military Police trained in Belgium-
officer badge.
Manufactured in Belgium.
Size: 12.0 cm X 4.5 cm.
Item #II-55.

PARACHUTIST, SAUDI ARABIA - 1960's
Cloth, embroidered with white wings on red
background and white border stitching. Worn
by Royal Military Police trained in Belgium.
Enlisted badge.
Manufactured in Belgium.
Size: 12.0 cm X 4.5 cm.
Item #II-56.

PARACHUTIST, SAUDI ARABIA - 1960's
Cloth, embroidered with gold wings on black
background and yellow border stitching. Worn
by officers who attained basic qualification.
Training conducted in Belgium.
Manufactured in Belgium.
Size: 12.0 cm X 4.5 cm.
Item #II-57.

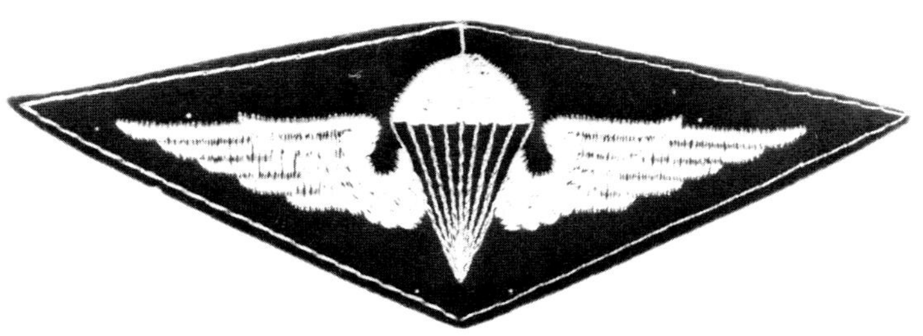

PARACHUTIST, SAUDI ARABIA - 1960's
Cloth, embroidered with white wings on black
background and white border stitching. Worn
by enlisted who attained basic qualification.
Training conducted in Belgium.
Manufactured in Belgium.
Size: 12.0 cm X 4.5 cm.
Item #II-58.

PARACHUTIST, SAUDI ARABIA - 1960's
Cloth embroidered with gold wings on a dark
green background and yellow border stitching.
Worn by officers who are commando course
graduates. Trained in Belgium.
Manufactured in Belgium.
Size: 12.o cm X 4.5 cm.
Item #II-59

PARACHUTIST, SAUDI ARABIA - 1960's
Cloth embroidered with white wings on a dark
green background and white border stitching.
Worn by enlisted personnel who are commando
course graduates. Trained in Belgium.
Manufactured in Belgium.
Size: 12.0 cm X 4.5 cm.
Item #II-60.

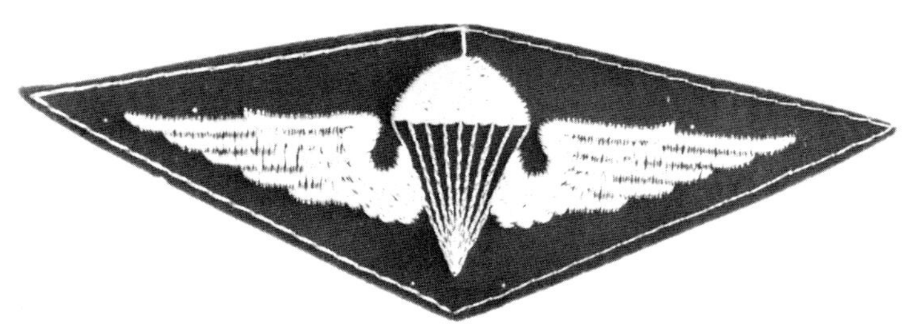

PARACHUTIST, SAUDI ARABIA - 1960's
Cloth embroidered with red wings on black
background and red border stitching. Worn
by officer & enlisted Royal Guard personnel
who were trained in Belgium.
Manufactured in Belgium.
Size: 12.0 cm X 4.5 cm.
Item #II-61.

PARACHUTIST, SAUDI ARABIA - 1970's
Silver metal, solid cast, with pin fastener.
Manufacturers stamp on reverse.
Manufactured in Egypt.
Size: 9.0 cm X 3.3 cm.
Item #II-63-A.

PARACHUTIST, BASIC, SAUDI ARABIA - 1970's
Silver metal, hollow stamped with pin
fastener. Worn by enlisted Saudis trained
in Egypt.
Manufactured in Egypt.
Size: 9.2 cm X 3.4 cm.
Item #II-63.

PARACHUTIST, 3rd Class, SAUDI ARABIA-1970's
Silver metal, hollow stamped, with pin
fastener. Worn by enlisted Saudis trained
in Egypt.
Manufactured in Egypt.
Size: 9.2 cm X 4.1 cm.
Item #II-64.

PARACHUTIST, 2nd Class, SAUDI ARABIA - 1970's
Silver metal, hollow stamped metal with pin
fastener. Worn by Saudis trained in Egypt -
enlisted personnel.
Manufactured in Egypt.
Size: 9.2 cm X 4.1 cm.
Item #II-65.

PARACHUTIST, 1st Class, SAUDI ARABIA - 1970's
Silver metal, hollow stamped, with pin fast-
ener. Worn by Saudi enlisted personnel
trained in Egypt.
Manufactured in Egypt.
Size: 9.2 cm X 4.5 cm.
Item #II-66.

PARACHUTIST, LAPEL PIN, SAUDI ARABIA - 1970's
Gold metal, stamped, lapel pin with pin
fastener.
Worn by officers and enlisted.
Manufactured in Egypt.
Size: 3.0 cm X 1.2 cm.
Item #II-62.

PARACHUTIST,SHOULDER LOOP ARCH, SAUDI
ARCH - 1970's.
Metal enameled shoulder loop arch with
arabic:AL-MEDALLAT(Parachutist). Red
background and gold writing. Manufactured
in Egypt.
Size: 6.8 cm X 2.4 cm.
Item #II-70.

PARACHUTIST, SHOULDER PATCH, SAUDI ARABIA
Cloth, embroidered shoulder sleeve patch
arch, with arabic: Selah Al-Medaliat Al-
Malaki Al-Saudi(Royal Saudi Parachute
Corps). Green background with white writ-
ing. Worn in the 1970's. Manuf. in Egypt.
Size: 11.4 cm X 3.1 cm.
Item #II-71.

COMMANDO, SLEEVE TAB, SAUDI ARABIA-1960's
Cloth embroidered sleeve tab, with arabic
Al-Seagah(Commando). Black background
with yellow writing. Manufactured in
Saudi Arabia.
Size: 6.2 cm X 2.4 cm.
Item #II-72.

COMMANDO, SLEEVE TAB, SAUDI ARABIA -1960s
Cloth embroidered sleeve tab, with arabic
AL-SEAGAH(Commando). Black background
with yellow writing. Manufactured in
Saudi Arabia.
Size: 7.6 cm X 3.4 cm.
Item #II-73.

COMMANDO, SHOULDER SLEEVE ARCH, SAUDI ARABIA-
1970's.
Metal enameled shoulder loop arch with arabic
writing: AL-SEAGAH(Commando). Gold writing on
black background, with pin clip fastener.
Manufactured in Egypt.
Size: 6.7 cm X 2.4 cm.
Item #II-74.

COMMANDO, SHOULDER SLEEVE ARCH, SAUDI ARABIA-
1970's.
Metal enameled shoulder loop arch with arabic
writing: AL-SEAGAH(Commando). Copper writing
on flat black background, with pin fastener.
Manufactured in Egypt.
Size: 6.8 cm X 2.2 cm.
Item #II-75.

AIRBORNE, BERET BADGE, SAUDI ARABIA-1960s
Gold metal beret badge worn by airborne
personnel.
Manufactured in Egypt.
Size: 4.0 cm X 6.0 cm.
Item #II-67.

AIRBORNE, BERET BADGE, SAUDI ARABIA-1970s
Green and gold metal beret badge worn by
airborne personnel.
Manufactured in Egypt.
Size: 3.9 cm X 4.5 cm.
Item #II-68.

AIRBORNE, BERET BADGE, SAUDI ARABIA-1980s
Gold metal beret badge worn by airborne
personnel.
Manufactured in the U.S.A.
Size: 4.2 cm diameter.
Item #II-69.

Item #II-70

Item #II-71

Item #II-72

Item #II-73

49

Item #II-74

Item #II-75

Item #II-76

Item #II-77

Item #II-78

Item #II-79

Item #II-80

Item #II-81

Item #II-82

Item #II-83

CAP, HAT AND BERET BADGES
CHAPTER III

The cap, hat and beret badges are all styled in such a way that the national symbol is incorporated into the design. The national symbol is a palm tree with crossed right sword over left sword below the palm tree and this is surrounded by a palm branch wreath with a royal crown at the top. Earlier designs have also included a scroll beneath the national symbol. On the scroll, written in arabic, will be the name of the particular organization. The presence of the scroll and arabic on these earlier badges helped to identify the respective organization or activity. The national symbol is a reminder to all Saudis of their heritage. The date palm tree, which traditionally, is the main agriculture crop, is symbolic of vitality and growth. The crossed swords, always unsheathed, symbolizes strength rooted in the faith of Islam. The palm branch wreath with royal crown at the top symbolizes the origin and strength of the Royal Family.

Army hats are of the western style with leather visors and metal hat badges. Army hats are worn with the service uniform and the formal or party uniform. The beret is the primary duty uniform headgear for Saudi Arabian Army personnel. The brown or OD beret is worn by the majority of the officers and enlisted personnel. However, specific beret colors are worn by various units and or specific branches.

Brown or OD colored Beret - Army recruits and most Army soldiers.

Bright Green Beret - Royal Palace Guard soldiers.

Bright Red Beret - Ministry of Defence and Aviation Military Police soldiers.

Dark Blue Beret - Air Defense Artillery soldiers.

Maroon Beret - Airborne soldiers

Black Beret - Armor soldiers

No badges are manufactured in Saudi Arabia. All of the various types or styles were manufactured in Egypt, Korea, Jordan, Taiwan, Middle Eastern Countries, or the United States of America. The current hat, beret, and cap badges are of a very high quality and well designed. The following pages show examples of the various hat, cap, and beret badges which were worn by the Saudi Army personnel over the past years.

BERET/CAP BADGE - 1950's & 1960's
Cast brass, slightly domed with green felt
backing. Arabic above and below swords.
Manufactured in the Middle East for Saudi
Arabia.
Size: 4.3 cm X 5.8 cm.
Item #III-1.

HAT BADGE - 1950's & 1960's
Cast brass, flat, gold metal. Arabic above
and below swords. Pin clip fastener.
Manufactured in the Middle East for Saudi
Arabia.
Size: 4.2 cm X 5.7 cm.

Item #III-2.

BERET/CAP BADGE - 1960's
Cast brass with gray wool backing.
Gold metal with pin clip fastener.
Manufactured in Egypt.
Size: 3.8 cm X 5.5 cm.
Item #III-3.

BERET/CAP BADGE - 1960's
Cast brass with pin fastener.
Manufactured in the Middle East
for Saudi Arabia.
Size: 4.0 cm X 5.6 cm.
Item #III-4.

HAT BADGE - 1960's
Cast flat brass with pin fastener.
Manufactured in Egypt for Saudi
Arabia.
Size: 4.2 cm X 5.8 cm.
Item #III-5.

HAT BADGE - 1960's
Cast flat aluminium with pin
fastener. Manufactured in the
Middle East for Saudi Arabia.
Size: 4.5 cm X 6.2 cm.
Item #III-6.

BERET BADGE - 1970's
Stamped brass with green back-
ground and gold painted raised
relief. Pin Clip fastener.
Manufactured in Egypt for Saudi
Arabia.
Size: 3.8 cm X 4.8 cm.
Item #III-7.

BERET BADGE - 1970's
Stamped brass with green back-
ground and raised silver relief.
Screw post fastener.
Manufactured in Egypt for Saudi
Arabia.
Size: 3.8 cm X 4.6 cm.
Item #III-8.

BERET BADGE - 1970's
Stamped brass with green enameled
background and brass relief. Pin
clip fastener.
Manufactured in the Middle East
for Saudi Arabia.
Size: 4.0 cm X 4.6 cm.
Item #III-9.

BERET BADGE - 1970's
Stamped brass with green painted
background and raised gold relief.
Pin clip fastener.
Manufactured in Egypt for Saudi
Arabia.
Size: 4.0 cm X 5.0 cm.
Item #III-10.

BERET BADGE - 1970's
Stamped brass with green painted
background and raised brass relief.
Pin clip fastener.
Manufactured in Egypt for Saudi
Arabia.
Size: 4.0 cm X 4.7 cm.
Item #III-11.

BERET BADGE - 1970's
Stamped brass with green back-
ground and silver raised relief.
Screw post fastener.
Manufactured in Korea.
Size: 4.0 cm X 4.5 cm.
Item #III-12.

HAT BADGE - 1970's
Stamped alloy with green enamel
background and bright brass raised
relief. Design error in swords.
Screw post fastener.
Manufactured in Korea.
Size: 4.7 cm X 6.7 cm.
Item #III-13.

HAT BADGE -1970's
Stamped brass, slightly domed. Green back-
ground and raised brass relief. Pin clip
fastener. Manufactured in Korea for Saudi
Arabia.
Size: 5.2 cm X 6.2 cm.
Item #III-14.

HAT BADGE - 1970's
Stamped brass, flat, with pin clip fastener.
Green background and brass relief.
Manufactured in the Middle East for Saudi
Arabia.
Size: 5.7 cm X 6.2 cm.
Item #III-15.

HAT BADGE - 1970's
Stamped brass, flat, with pin clip fastener.
Green backgound and brass raised relief.
Manufactured in Egypt for Saudi Arabia.
Size: 5.5 cm X 6.5 cm.
Item #III-16.

BERET BADGE - 1980's
Two piece, stamped brass, slightly domed.
Screw post fastener.
Manufactured in the U.S.A.
Size: 4.2 cm diameter.
Item #III-17.

BERET BADGE - 1980's
Two piece, stamped brass, slightly domed.
Screw post fastener.
Manufactured in Taiwan or Korea for Saudi
Arabia.
Size: 4.5 cm diameter.
Item #III-18.

BERET BADGE - 1980's
Two piece stamped brass, slightly domed with
screw post fastener.
Manufactured in Egypt for Saudi Arabia.
Size: 4.0 cm diameter.
Item #III-19.

HAT BADGE - 1980's
One piece stamped brass with pin clip fastener.
Manufactured in Egypt for Saudi Arabia.
Size: 4.8 cm diameter.
Item #III-20.

HAT BADGE - 1980's
Two piece stamped brass with screw post
fastener.
Manufactured in Taiwan or Korea.
Size: 4.5 cm diameter.
Item #III-21.

HAT BADGE - 1980's
Two piece stamped brass with screw post
fastener. Slightly domed.
Manufactured in the U.S.A. for Saudi Arabia.
Size: 5.0 cm diameter.
Item #III-22.

ROYAL SAUDI ARMED FORCES VEHICLE PLATE-1950's
Brass, solid cast, with early period national
symbol for Armed Forces.
Manufactured in Saudi Arabia.
Size: 12,0 cm X 12.0 cm.
Item #III-23.

Item #III-24

Item #III-25

Item #III-26

Item #III-27

Item #III-28

Item #III-29

Item #III-30

Enlisted chevrons or stripes, during the 1950's, were primarily a cloth type that was pinned on the shirt sleeve. Some five different patterns were used. Some of which were actually made by local tailors.

In the 1960's and early 1970's, the material and color was standardized. The stripes were of a green satin material sewn on OD wool. Stripes were usually only pinned on the shirt sleeve.

By the late 1970's, the stripes were of the Swiss loom embroidered type with merrowed edges. Stripes are now sewn on uniform sleeves by sewing machine or attached by snaps.

The warrant officer rank is currently like a gold lieutenants bar. The warrant officer rank is worn on the shoulder loop or epaulet.

Outstanding non-commissioned officers are promoted by progression to warrant officer ranks. Very few NCO's or warrant officers cross over to the commissioned officer ranks. The objective of building a highly skilled NCO and Warrant Officer Technician base is reflected in the high monetary rewards which these soldiers receive.

The following pages illustrate the various types of enlisted insignia of rank badges that have been developed over the years.

PRE - 1980's

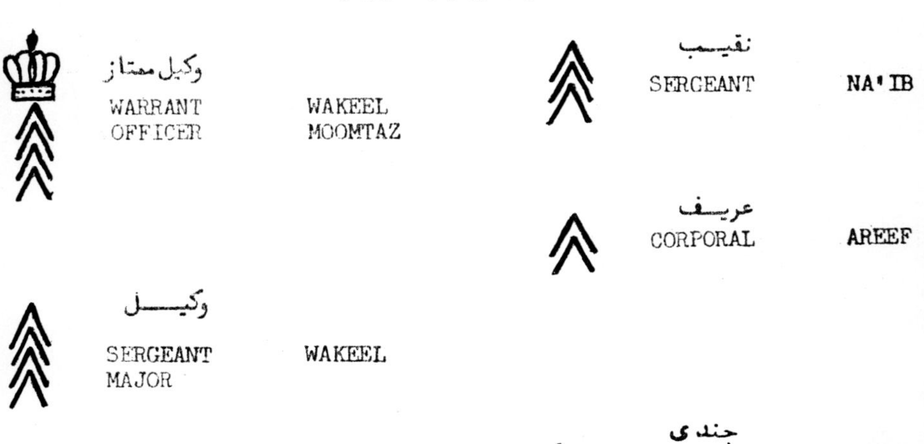

MASTER SERGEANT – Worn in 1950/60s
Army – Green felt stripes on khaki
cotton.
Manufactured in the Middle East.
Size: 12.8 cm X 9.9 cm.
Item #IV-1.

SERGEANT - Worn in the 1950/60's
Army - Green felt stripes on khaki
cotton.
Manufactured in the Middle East.
Size: 11.0 cm X 8.5 cm.
Item #IV-2.

MASTER SERGEANT - Worn in 1950/60s
Army, Air Defense - Black satin
stripes on Khaki cotton.
Manufactured in the Middle East.
Size: 11.5 cm X 11.4 cm.
Item #IV-3.

CORPORAL - Worn in 1950/60's
Army, Air Defense - Black felt on
OD green cotton.
Manufactured in the Middle East.
Size: 10.4 cm X 9.6 cm.
Item #IV-4.

SERGEANT - Worn in 1950/60's
Army - Green felt stripes on khaki
cotton.
Manufactured in the Middle East.
Size: 11.2 cm X 10.0 cm.
Item #IV-5.

MASTER SERGEANT - Worn in 1960/70s
Army - Green satin stripes on OD
wool.
Manufactured in the Middle East.
Size: 10.5 cm X 8.2 cm.
Item #IV-6.

SERGEANT - Worn in the 1950/60's
Army - Green satin stripes on OD
wool.
Manufactured in the Middle East.
Size: 10.8 cm X 7.5 cm.
Item #IV-7.

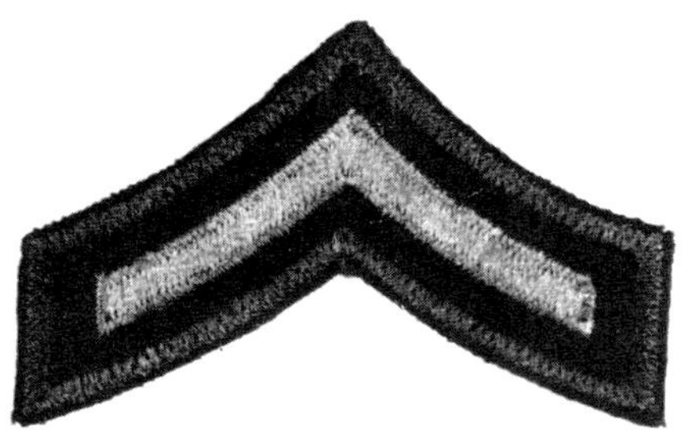

LANCE CORPORAL - Worn in 1980's
Army - Green stripe on brown felt.
Swiss loom type embroidery.
Manufactured in the U.S.A. for
Saudi Arabia.
Size: 8.0 cm X 5.0 cm.
Item #IV-8.

CORPORAL - Worn in the 1980's
Army - Green stripes on brown
felt. Swiss loom type embroidery.
Manufactured in the U.S.A. for
Saudi Arabia.
Size: 8 0 cm X 6.5 cm.
Item #IV-9.

SERGEANT - Worn in the 1980's
Army - Green stripes on brown
felt. Swiss loom type embroidery.
Manufactured in the U.S.A. for
Saudi Arabia.
Size: 8.0 cm X 7.5 cm.
Item #IV-10.

FIRST SERGEANT - Worn in the 1980s
Army - Green stripes on brown felt.
Swiss loom type embroidery.
Manufactured in the U.S.A. for
Saudi Arabia.
Size: 8.0 cm X 8.7 cm.
Item #IV-11.

MASTER SERGEANT - Worn in 1980's
Army - Green stripes on brown felt.
Swiss loom type embroidery.
Manufactured in the U.S.A. for
Saudi Arabia.
Size: 8.0 cm X 8.7 cm.
Item #IV-12.

SERGEANT MAJOR - Worn in 1980's
Army - Green stripes on brown felt.
Swiss loom type embroidery.
Manufactured in the U.S.A. for
Saudi Arabia.
Size: 8.0 cm X 9.3 cm.
Item #IV-13.

WARRANT OFFICER - Worn in 1970/80s
Army - Gold metal bar with pin
post fastners.
Manufactured in Western Europe.
Size: 1.0 cm X 3.0 cm.
Item #IV-14.

Item #IV-15.

Item #IV-16.

Item #IV-17

Item #IV-18

Item #IV-19

Item #IV-20

Item #IV-21

Item #IV-22

Item #IV-23

Item #IV-24

Item #IV-25

Item #IV-26

Item #IV-27

Item #IV-28

Item #IV-29

Item #IV-30

OFFICER RANK BADGES
CHAPTER V

The Saudi Arabian Army officer rank components such as the star, crown and crossed swords have remained essentially the same over the past 30 years, with only slight variations. The current star is larger, with a smaller national symbol in the center, than the previous star. The current crown has a much smoother appearance. The current crossed swords are also more elegant in appearance.

In 1976, the warrant officer rank was changed from four chevrons and a crown, worn on the sleeve, to a gold bar worn on the shoulder loops. Also in 1978, the rank of Major General was changed from a crossed sword and star to a crossed sword and crown. Lieutenant General was changed from crossed swords and crown to a crossed sword, star and crown. General was changed from crossed sword, star and crown to a crossed sword, two stars and a crown. The Field Marshal rank, which was crossed sword, baton, wreath, and crown was eliminated.

In 1979, slip-on shoulder epaulet ranks were being introduced in the commerical uniform shops. These slip-on shoulder board ranks were embroidered in gold bullion and green satin thread. They are being manufactured by hand in Pakistan. Some slip-on types are available with only the arch(arabic writing) embroidered and others which are just plain tan slip-on's to which the officer can affix his metal rank badges and the metal arch.

The following pages illustrate the various officer rank badges and the variations of stars, crowns, and swords.

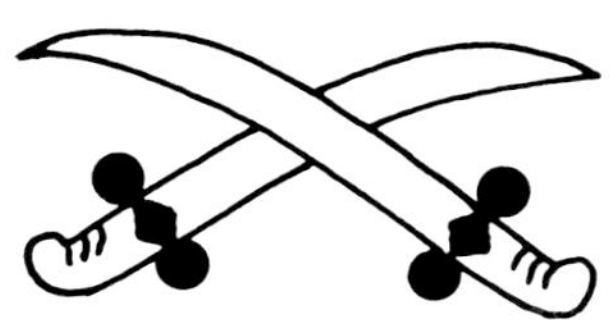

STAR RANK BADGE - 1950's & 1960s
Brass with raised sword and palm
design in center. Component of
officers rank.
Manufactured in Egypt for Saudi
Arabia. Loops for attaching.
Size: 2.5 cm diameter.
Item #V-1.

STAR RANK BADGE - 1960's
Brass and enamel with green
center. National symbol in center
Manufactured in Egypt for Saudi
Arabia. Loops for attaching.
Size: 2.5 cm diameter.
Item #V-2.

STAR RANK BADGE - 1970's
Brass and green enamel center
with national symbol. Pin post
fastener.
Manufactured in the Middle East
for Saudi Arabia.
Size: 2.5 cm diameter.
Item #V-3.

STAR RANK BADGE - 1970's
Brass and green enamel center
with national symbol. Pin post
fastener.
Manufactured in Egypt for Saudi
Arabia.
Size: 2.5 cm diameter.
Item #V-4.

STAR RANK BADGE - 1970's
Brass and green enamel center
with national symbol. Pin post
fastener.
Manufactured in Korea for Saudi
Arabia.
Size: 2.6 cm diameter.
Item #V-5.

STAR RANK BADGE - 1970's
Aluminium with green center and
national symbol. Pin post fast-
ener.
Manufactured in Europe for Saudi
Arabia.
Size: 2.4 cm diameter.
Item #V-6.

STAR RANK BADGE - 1980's
Brass with green enameled center
and national symbol. Screw post
fastener.
Manufactured in Korea for Saudi
Arabia.
Size: 2.6 cm diameter.
Item #V-7.

STAR RANK BADGE - 1980's
Brass with recessed green enamel-
ed center and national symbol.
Pin post fastener.
Manufactured in Taiwan.
Size: 2.5 cm diameter.
Item #V-7.

STAR RANK BADGE - 1980's
Brass with recessed green enamel-
ed center and national symbol.
Pin post fastener.
Manufactured in the U.S.A.
Size: 2.7 cm diameter.
Item #V-8.

Item #V-9.

CROWN RANK BADGE - 1960's
Brass with green painted back-
ground. Pin post fastener.
Worn by field grade officers &
above.
Manufactured in the Middle East.
Size: 3.0 cm X 2.5 cm.
Item #V-10.

CROWN RANK BADGE - 1960's
Brass with green painted back-
ground. Pin post fastener.
Manufactured in Egypt.
Size: 2.8 cm X 2.5 cm.
Item #V-11.

CROWN RANK BADGE - 1970's
Brass with green enamel back-
ground. Worn by field grade off-
icers and above. Loop fastener.
Manufactured in Egypt for Saudi
Arabia.
Size: 3.0 cm X 2.5 cm.
Item #V-12.

CROWN RANK BADGE - 1970's
Aluminum , gold plated with
green painted background. Pin
post fastener.
Manufactured in Europe for Saudi
Arabia.
Size: 3.0 cm X 2.6 cm.
Item #V-13.

CROWN RANK BADGE - 1980's
Brass with green enameled back-
ground. Pin clip fastener.
Manufactured in the U.S.A.
Size: 3.0 cm X 2.4 cm.
Item #V-14.

Item #V-15.

FIELD MARSHAL, SHOULDER BOARD
RANK BADGE - Pre-1975
Red felt with gold bullion
wreath, crown, sword, & baton.
NOT CURRENTLY USED- Arabic:
Musheer. Manufactured in Pakistan
Size: 6.5 cm X 8.4 cm.
Item #V-16.

CROSSED SWORDS RANK BADGE-1960's
Cast brass with right sword over
left sword. Manufactured in the
Middle East for Saudi Arabia.
Loop type fastener.
Size: 5.5 cm X 4.0 cm.
Item #V-17.

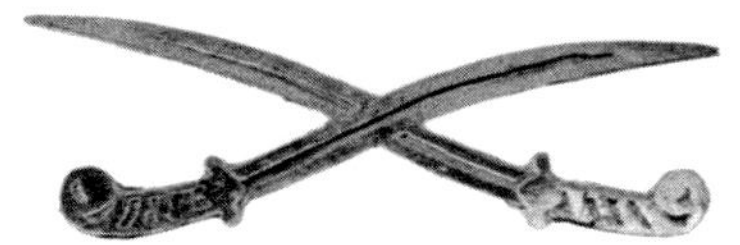

CROSSED SWORDS RANK BADGE-1970's
Stamped brass with loop fastener
Swords in error.
Manufactured in Egypt.
Size: 4.5 cm X 1.5 cm.
Item #V-18.

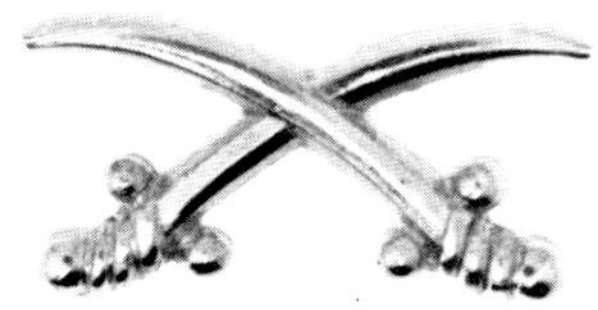

CROSSED SWORDS RANK BADGE-1980's
Stamped brass with pin fastener.
Worn by MG & above. Manufactured
in Egypt, Korea, and U.S.A.
Size: 3.8 cm X 2.0 cm.
Item #V-19.

Item #V-20.

SLIP-ON SHOULDER BOARD -1960/70's
Cloth, tan background with red
stripe. Worn by senior students
at KAA Military Academy.
Manufactured in the Middle East.
Size: 5.7 cm X 7.9 cm.
Item #V-21.

SLIP-ON RANK SHOULDER BOARD-1960s
Dark brown wool with red and
gold bullion star.
Manufactured in the Middle East.
Size: 6.2 cm X 9.9 cm.
Item #V-22.

SLIP-ON RANK SHOULDER BOARD-1980's
Cloth, tan with green and gold
bullion star and national symbol.
Manufactured in Pakistan.
Size: 7.0 cm X 8.4 cm.
Item #V-23.

SLIP-ON RANK SHOULDER BOARD-1980's
Tan cloth, with green & gold
bullion stars and arabic writing.
Rank is captain. Manufactured in
Pakistan. Size: 6.8cm X 13cm.
Item #V-24.(Captain)

SLIP-ON RANK SHOULDER BOARD-1980's
Tan cloth, with green & gold
bullion stars and crown with
arabic writing:Saudi Arabian
Army. Manufactured in Pakistan.
Size: 7.2 cm X 11.9 cm.
Item #V-25 (Colonel)

SLIP-ON RANK SHOULDER BOARD-1980s
Tan cloth, with green and gold
bullion crown and sword.
Manufactured in Pakistan.
Size: 7.1 cm X 11.6 cm.
Item #V-26.(Major General)

SLIP-ON RANK SHOULDER BOARD-1980s
Tan cloth, with green and gold
bullion crown, star, and arabic
writing.
Manufactured in Pakistan.
Size: 6.7 cm X 11.0 cm.
Item #V-27.(Lieutenant Colonel)

SECOND LIEUTENANT	LIEUTENANT	CAPTAIN
MULAZIM THANI	MULAZIM AWWAL	RA'EES or NAGIBE
Item #V-29	Item #V-30	Item #V-31
MAJOR	LIEUTENANT COLONEL	COLONEL
WAKEEL QAYED	QA'ID	AQ'EED
Item #V-32	Item #V-33	Item #V-34

BRIGADIER
GENERAL

ZA'EEM

Item #V-35

MAJOR
GENERAL

LEWA'

Item #V-36

LIEUTENANT
GENERAL

FAREEK
THANI

Item #V-37

GENERAL

FAREEK
OWWAL

Item #V-38

Item #V-39

Item #V-40

Item #V-41

Item #V-42

Item #V-43

Item #V-44

Item #V-45

Item #V-46

Item #V-47

Item #V-48

The Senior Officer Collar Tabs, which the British refer to as Gorget Patches, are worn by Colonels and above only.

These red and gold embroidered tabs or patches are worn on the right and left collar and attached by small metal snaps.

The tabs are manufactured in Pakistan for the duty uniform and in the U.S.A. for the party or formal uniform.

The following pages illustrate the three groups of Senior Officer Collar Tabs for the duty uniform and the formal or party uniform.

SENIOR OFFICER COLLAR TABS/GORGET PATCHES-70's
Red felt with silver bullion and gold button.
Worn by full Colonels.
Manufactured in Pakistan for Saudi Arabia.
Size: 3.5 cm X 6.7 cm.
Item #VI-1 and #VI-2.

SENIOR OFFICER COLLAR TABS/GORGET PATCHES-70's
Red felt with gold bullion and gold button.
Worn by Brig. Gen., Maj.Gen. & Lt. Gen.
Manufactured in Pakistan for Saudi Arabia.
Size: 3.5 cm X 8.2 cm.
Item #VI-3 and #VI-4.

SENIOR OFFICER COLLAR TABS/GORGET PATCHES-70's
Red felt with gold bullion and gold button.
Worn by full General.
Manufactured in Pakistan for Saudi Arabia.
Size: 3.7 cm X 8.5 cm.
Item #VI-5 and #VI-6.

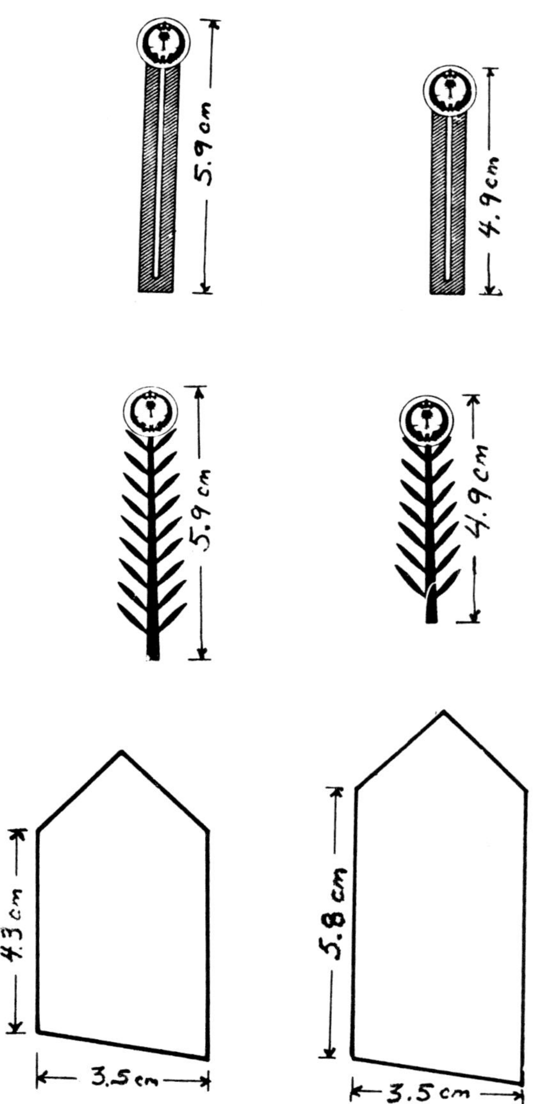

SENIOR OFFICER COLLAR TABS/GORGET PATCHES-80's
U.S. manufactured collar tabs/gorget patches.
Item #VI-7, VI-8 & VI-9(Left illustration for
duty uniform.)
Item #VI-10, VI-11 & VI-12(Right illustration
for formal or party uniform.)

As the Saudi Arabian Army began to modernize, the internal structure of the Army changed. The number of branches grew from nine to fifteen branches. The sophistication of modern defensive weapons dictates an internal organization that is capable of handling the many facets of training, logistics, operations and personnel. The current branches in the Saudi Arabian Army are considered capable of supporting the Kingdom of Saudi Arabia's defensive policies.

The branch insignia has gone through an evolution over the past 20-25 years as have the other types of insignia. Some branches have been more aggressive, in terms of insignia design or modification, than others. Some branches like the Royal Guard, have been eliminated. In the case of the Royal Guard, in the spring of 1964, it was incorporated into the Regular Army as an infantry unit. This elite force of some 4,000 officers and men became the base elements for new combat units.

Other branches just seemed to disappear in terms of insignia, but their missions were absorbed by another branch or a number of branches.

All branch insignia is manufactured in other countries such as Egypt, Jordan, Syria, Korea, United Kingdom, or the United Sates of America.

The current branch insignia clearly depicts the function of the particular branch. This new insignia was adopted in 1978 and is very well made and of high quality craftsmanship. Issued in pairs, a number of branches have right and left collar versions. Officers, warrants, and enlisted personnel all wear the same insignia for their respective branch.

Some of the early branch insignia was adopted directly from the Egyptian Armed Forces, but modified to reflect it as Saudi Arabian insignia.

The following pages illustrate the various branch of service badges over the years.

AIR DEFENSE ARTILLERY BRANCH BADGE
Worn in the 1960's. Silver metal
with pin clip fastener. Right &
Left types. Manufactured in
Europe.
Size: 3.0 cm diameter.
Item #VII-1 and #VII-2.

AIR DEFENSE ARTILLERY BRANCH BADGE
Worn in the 1970's. Gold metal
with pin post fastener. Hawk missile
on badge. Right and Left types.
Manufactured in Egypt.
Size: 4.0 cm X 2.6 cm.
Item #VII-3 and #VII-4.
(No illustration available)

AIR DEFENSE ARTILLERY BRANCH BADGE
Worn in the 1980's. Brass, two-
piece, bright type. Right and
left types. Officer & enlisted.
Manufactured in U.S.A. & Korea.
Pin type-U.S.A.;Screw type-Korea.
Size: 2.8 cm diameter.
Item #VII-5 and #VII-6.

ARMOR BRANCH BADGE – Worn in 1950's.
Gold cast metal with pin clip
fastener. Light Armor branch.
Manufactured in Syria for Saudi
Arabia.
Size: 2.4 cm X 3.4 cm.
Item #VII-7.

ARMOR BRANCH BADGE – Worn in 1960's
Brass cast metal with pin clip
fastener. Right and Left types.
Manufactured in Syria for Saudi
Arabia.
Size: 2.5 cm X 2.4 cm.
Item #VII-8 and #VII-9.

ARMOR BRANCH BADGE -Worn in 1970's.
Stamped brass with pin clip fast-
ener. Right and Left types.
Manufactured in Egypt for Saudi
Arabia.
Size: 3.0 cm X 2.6 cm.
Item #VII-10 and #VII-11.

ARMOR BRANCH BADGE - Worn in 1980's
Brass, two-piece, bright type.
Worn by officer & enlisted.
Manufactured in U.S.A(Pin Post)
and Korea(Screw Post).
Size: 2.8 cm diameter.
Item #VII-12.

ARTILLERY BRANCH BADGE-Worn in 50's
Brass & subdued color - cast type.
Loops for fastening.
Manufactured in Middle East for
Saudi Arabia.
Size: 2.0 cm X 3.0 cm.
Item #VII-13(brass) & #VII-14(Sub-
dued)

ARTILLERY BRANCH BADGE-Worn in 60's
Brass, cast type with pin clip
fastener. Dark gold color.
Manufactured in Egypt for Saudi
Arabia.
Size: 2.5cm X 3.4cm.
Item #VII-15.

ARTILLERY BRANCH BADGE-Worn in 70's
Stamped, bright gold color with
pin post fastener.
Manufactured in Egypt for Saudi
Arabia.
Size: 2.2 cm X 3.7 cm.
Item #VII-16.

ARTILLERY BRANCH BADGE-Worn in 80's.
Brass, two-piece, stamped, bright
type. Worn by officers & enlisted.
Manufactured in U.S.A.(Pin Post) &
Korea(Screw Post).
Size: 2.8 cm diameter.
Item #VII-17.

BAND BRANCH BADGE - Worn in 1980's
Brass, two-piece, stamped, bright
type. Worn by officers & enlisted.
Manufactured in U.S.A.(Pin post) &
Korea(Screw post).
Size: 2.8 cm diameter.
Item #VII-18.

Item #VII-19.

CHEMICAL BRANCH BADGE - Worn in 60's
Silver, cast with pin clip fastner.
Eliminated from list of branches
in mid- 1960's. Manufactured in
Egypt for Saudi Arabia.
Size: 3.4 cm X 3.1 cm.
Item #VII-20.

ENGINEER BRANCH BADGE-Worn in 50's
Brass, cast type, gold color with
pin clip fastener.
Manufactured in Syria for Saudi
Arabia.
Size: 2.3 cm X 3.3 cm.
Item #VII-21.

ENGINEER BRANCH BADGE-Worn in 50's
Silver, cast type with pin clip
fastener.
Manufactured in the Middle East.
Size: 2.2 cm X 3.3 cm.
Item #VII-22.

ENGINEER BRANCH BADGE-Worn in 70's
Gold, stamped type with pin clip
fastener.
Manufactured in Egypt for Saudi
Arabia.
Size: 2.4 cm X 3.8 cm.
Item #VII-23.

ENGINEER BRANCH BADGE-Worn in 80's
Brass, two-piece, stamped, bright
type. Worn by officers & enlisted.
Manufactured in U.S.A.(Pin post) &
Korea(Screw post).
Size: 2.8 cm diameter.
Item #VII-24.

INFANTRY BRANCH BADGE-Worn in 50's
Brass, solid cast with loop fast-
ener.
Manufactured in the Middle East.
Size: 3.7 cm X 2.2 cm.
Item #VII-25.

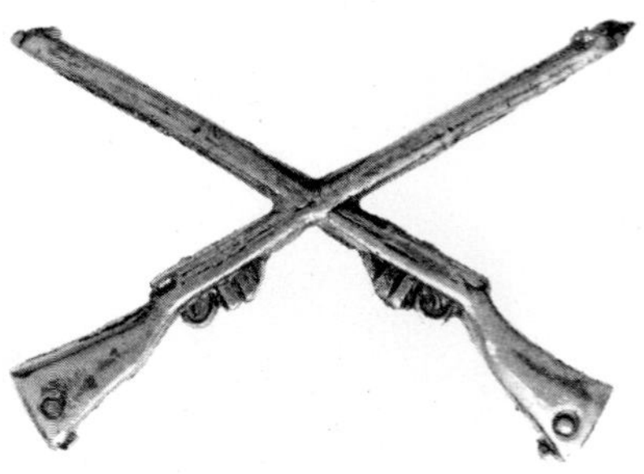

INFANTRY BRANCH BADGE-Worn in 50's
Brass, solid cast with loop fast-
ener.
Manufactured in the Middle East for
Saudi Arabia.
Size: 5.4 cm X 3.8 cm.
Item #VII-26.

INFANTRY BRANCH BADGE-Worn in 60's
Brass, solid stamped with pin clip
fastener. Right & Left type with
cresent & three stars.
Manufactured in Egypt.
Size: 2.6 cm X 3.5 cm.
Item #VII-27 and #VII-28.

INFANTRY BRANCH BADGE-Worn in 60's
Brass, solid stamped with pin post
fastener. Right & Left type with
royal crown.
Manufactured in Middle East for
Saudi Arabia.
Size: 2.6 cm X 3.6 cm.
Item #VII-29 and #VII-30.

INFANTRY BRANCH BADGE-Worn in 70's
Brass, solid stamped with pin clip
fastener. Right and Left type with
royal crown.
Manufactured in Egypt for Saudi
Arabia.
Size: 2.8 cm X 4.5 cm.
Item #VII-31 and #VII-32.

INFANTRY BRANCH BADGE-Worn in 80's
Brass, hollow stamped with pin
clip fastener. New design.
Manufactured in Egypt.
Size: 2.9 cm diameter.
Item #VII-33.

INFANTRY BRANCH BADGE-Worn in 80's
Brass, two-piece, solid stamped.
Right and Left types.
Manufactured in U.S.A.(Pin post)
and Korea(Screw post) for Saudi
Arabia.
Size: 2.8 cm diameter.
Item #VII-34 and #VII-35.

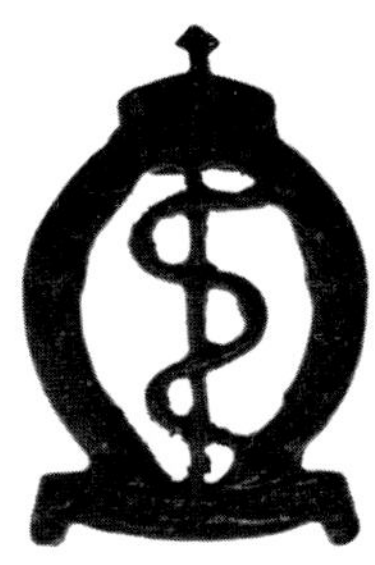

MEDICAL BRANCH BADGE-Worn in 60's
Brass, subdued, solid stamped with
pin clip fastener. Worn by all
medical & dental personnel.
Manufactured in Egypt for Saudi
Arabia.
Size: 2.2 cm X 3.4 cm.
Item #VII-36.

MEDICAL BRANCH BADGE-Worn in 70's
Brass, solid stamped with pin clip
fastener. Worn by all medical &
dental personnel.
Manufactured in Egypt for Saudi
Arabia.
Size: 2.4 cm X 3.6 cm.
Item #VII-37.

MEDICAL BRANCH BADGE-Worn in 80's
Brass, two-piece, solid stamped.
Worn by all medical & dental per-
sonnel.
Manufactured in the U.S.A.(Pin post
and Korea(Screw post) for Saudi
Arabia.
Size: 2.8 cm diameter Item #VII-38.

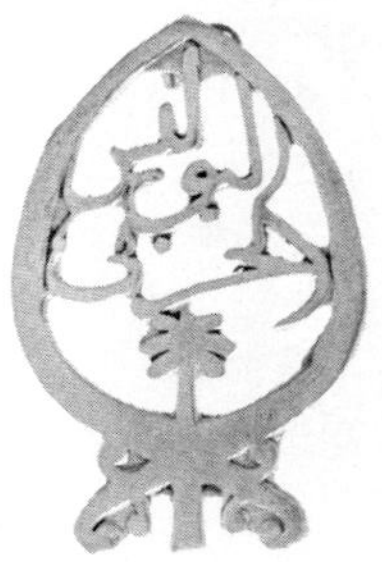

MILITARY POLICE BRANCH BADGE-1950's
Brass, solid stamp with pin clip
fastener.
Manufactured in the Middle East.
Size: 2.4 cm X 3.9 cm.
Item #VII-39.

MILITARY POLICE BRANCH BADGE-1960's
Brass, solid stamp with pin clip
fastener.
Manufactured in Egypt for Saudi
Arabia.
Size: 2.2 cm X 3.6 cm.
Item #VII-40.

MILITARY POLICE BRANCH BADGE-1970's
Brass, solid stamp with pin clip
fastener.
Manufactured in Egypt.
Size: 2.6 cm X 3.9 cm.
Item #VII-41.

MILITARY POLICE BRANCH BADGE-1980's
Brass, two-piece, solid stamped.
Right and Left types.
Manufactured in U.S.A.(Pin post)
and Korea(Screw post) for Saudi
Arabia.
Size: 2.8 cm diameter.
Item #VII-42 and #VII-43.

MILITARY SURVEY BRANCH BADGE-1980's

NO ILLUSTRATION AVAILABLE

Item #VII-44.

MILITARY INTELLIGENCE BRANCH
BADGE - 1980's

NO ILLUSTRATION AVAILABLE

Item #VII-45.

ORDNANCE BRANCH BADGE-Worn in 70's
Brass, solid stamped with pin clip
fastener.
Manufactured in Egypt for Saudi
Arabia.
Size: 2.3 cm X 3.5 cm.
Item #VII-46.

ORDNANCE BRANCH BADGE-Worn in 70's
Brass, solid stamped, light metal
with pin clip fastener.
Manufactured in the Middle East.
Size: 2.2 cm X 3.3 cm.
Item #VII-47.

ORDNANCE BRANCH BADGE-Worn in 1980's
Brass, two-piece, solid stamped.
Worn by officers & enlisted.
Manufactured in U.S.A.(Pin post)
and Korea(Screw post) for Saudi
Arabia.
Size: 2.8 cm diameter.
Item #VII-48.

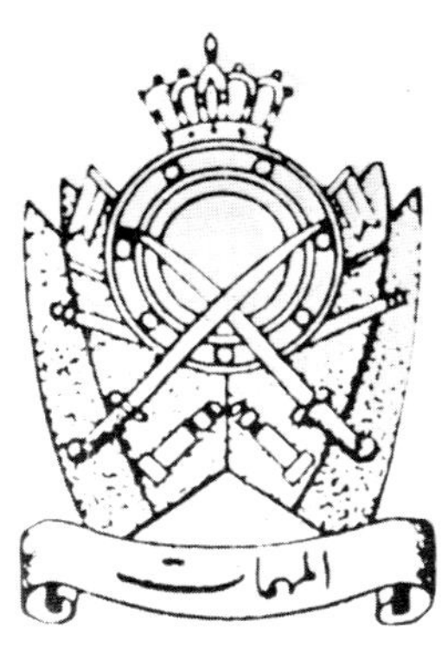

QUARTERMASTER BRANCH BADGE-1970's
Brass, solid stamped with pin clip
fastener.
Manufactured in Egypt for Saudi
Arabia.
Size: 2.6 cm X 3.9 cm.
Item #VII-49.

QUARTERMASTER BRANCH BADGE-1980's
Brass, two-piece, solid stamped.
Right and Left types.
Manufactured in U.S.A.(Pin post)
and Korea(Screw post) for Saudi
Arabia.
Size: 2.8 cm diameter.
Item #VII-50 and #VII-51.

RELIGIOUS AFFAIRS BRANCH BADGE-80's
Two-piece, brass, solid stamped.
Manufactured in U.S.A.(Pin post)
and Korea(Screw post) for Saudi
Arabia. Right and Left types.
Size: 2.8 cm diameter.
Item #VII-52 and #VII-53.

ROYAL GUARD BRANCH BADGE-1950-64.
Brass, solid stamped with pin
clip fastener. Branch incorporated
into Infantry in 1964.
Manufactured in Egypt for Saudi
Arabia.
Size: 3.9 cm X 5.0 cm.
Item #VII-54.

ROYAL GUARD BRANCH BADGE-1950's
Brass, solid stamped with pin
clip fastener.
Manufactured in Egypt.
Size: 2.5 cm X 3.4 cm.
Item #VII-55.

SERVICES/ADMINISTRATION BRANCH
BADGE - Worn in 1960's
Brass, solid stamped, with pin
clip fastener. Cresent and 3 stars.
Branch eliminated in 1970's.
Manufactured in Egypt.
Size: 2.6 cm X 3.0 cm.
Item #VII-56.

SERVICES/ADMINISTRATION BRANCH
BADGE - Worn in 1970's.
Brass, solid stamped, with pin
clip fastener. Branch eliminated in
1970's.
Manufactured in Egypt for Saudi
Arabia.
Size: 3.0 cm diameter. Item#VII-57.

SERVICES/ADMINISTRATION BRANCH
BADGE - Worn in 1970's.
Silver, solid stamped, with pin
clip fastener. Branch eliminated in
1970's. Manufactured in Egypt for
Saudi Arabia. Size: 3 cm diameter.
Item #VII-58.

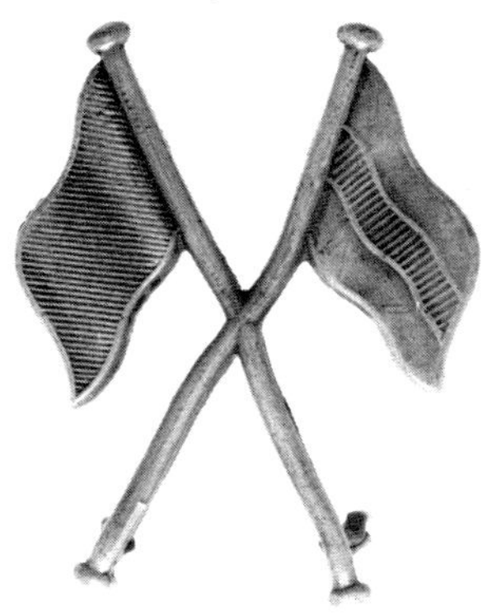

SIGNAL CORPS BRANCH BADGE-1950's
Solid cast, brass, with loop fast-
ener.
Manufactured in the Middle East.
Size: 4.0 cm X 5.0 cm.
Item #VII-59.

SIGNAL CORPS BRANCH BADGE-1950's
Solid cast, brass, with loop fast-
ener. Flag variation.
Manufactured in the Middle East.
Size: 3.7 cm X 5.0 cm.
Item #VII-60.

SIGNAL CORPS BRANCH BADGE-1960's
Brass, solid cast metal with pin
clip fastener.
Manufactured in Egypt for Saudi
Arabia.
Size: 2.4 cm X 3.5 cm.
Item #VII-61.

SIGNAL CORPS BRANCH BADGE-1960's
Brass, solid cast metal with pin
clip fastener.
Manufactured in Egypt for Saudi
Arabia.
Size: 2.4 cm X 3.5 cm.
Item #VII-62.

SIGNAL CORPS BRANCH BADGE-1960's
Brass, solid stamped, with pin
clip fastener.
Manufactured in Egypt for Saudi
Arabia.
Size: 2.3 cm X 3.8 cm.
Item #VII-63.

SIGNAL CORPS BRANCH BADGE-1970's
Brass, solid stamped, with pin
clip fastener. Flag design changed
Manufactured in Egypt for Saudi
Arabia.
Size: 3.4 cm X 4.4 cm.
Item #VII-64.

SIGNAL CORPS BRANCH BADGE-1980's
Brass, hollow stamped, with pin
clip fastener. New design.
Manufactured in Egypt.
Size: 2.9 cm diameter.
Item #VII-65.

SIGNAL CORPS BRANCH BADGE-1980's
Brass, two-piece, solid stamped
with pin post(USA) and screw
post(Korea) fastner.
Manufactured in U.S.A. & Korea.
Size: 2.8 cm diameter.
Item #VII-66 and #VII-67.

TRANSPORTATION BRANCH BADGE-1960's
Silver, solid stamped with pin
clip fastener. Design adopted by
Ordnance Corps in late 1960's.
Manufactured in Egypt.
Size: 2.5 cm X 3.0 cm.
Item #VII-68.

TRANSPORTATION BRANCH BADGE-1980's
Brass, two-piece, solid stamped
with pin post(USA) and screw
post(Korea) fastner.
Manufactured in U.S.A. & Korea.
Size: 2.8 cm diameter.
Item #VII-69 and #VII-70.

Item #VII-71

Item #VII-72

Item #VII-73

Item #VII-74

Item #VII-75

Item #VII-76

Item #VII-77

Item #VII-78

Item #VII-79

Item #VII-80

Item #VII-81

Item #VII-82

Item #VII-83

Item #VII-84

Item #VII-85

Item #VII-86

Item #VII-87

Item #VII-88

Item #VII-89

Item #VII-90

SHOULDER PATCHES AND ARCHES
CHAPTER VIII

In the late 1950's and 1960's, most soldiers wore shoulde
sleeve patches sewn on each shoulder sleeve of the shirt.
These patches indicated the type of organization to which he
was assigned, such as a military school or in some cases a
particular branch. Patches were also developed for units
assigned to a particular security region.

Beginning in the late 1960's and extending into the
1970's, special shoulder patches were designed and produced
which reflected current attendance at the military academy or
joint staff college.

Some pocket patches were also developed in the late
1970's for U.S. personnel assigned as advisors or represent-
atives to Saudi military organizations as well as U.S. personnel assigned to U.S. government projects.

The French advisors had a shoulder sleeve patch for
their Military Mission and a pocket badge for those personnel
assigned to the Saudi Armor Corps.

A large variety of materials and various countries were
involved in manufacturing these patches and arches.

Shoulder loop arches, which replaced most shoulder
patches, were a fairly recent uniforminsignia addition. These
archs are worn on the shoulder loop or epaulet of the officers
or enlisted mans shirt. Since all uniforms are essentially
the same, the arch helps to distinguish a soldier from the
Saudi Arabian Army from one who is with the other military
or para-military organizations. One arch is worn on each
epaulet at the point where the epaulet joins the shoulder
sleeve.

The earlier archs were manufactured in Egypt with
raised arabic writing. However, the Army and National Guard
obtained theirs from Korea and all arabic writing is dis-
played in cut-out fashion. This change to archs has
eliminated the sew-on shoulder sleeve patch for the Army.
However, middle of the sleeve patches are still in existence
for selected schools and activities.

The following pages illustrate the various known
patches and arches.

SHOULDER PATCH/ARCH - SAUDI ARAB-
IAN ARMY - Worn in the 1960/70's.
White arabic words on green back-
ground.
Manufactured in the Middle East.
Size: 11.3 cm X 3.8 cm.
Item #VIII-1.

SHOULDER PATCH/ARCH - SAUDI ARAB-
IAN ARMY - Worn in the 1970's.
White arabic words on dark green
background with red border.
Manufactured in the Middle East.
Size: 11.5 cm X 3.0 cm.
Item #VIII-2.

SHOULDER PATCH/ARCH - SAUDI ARAB-
IAN ARMY - Worn in the 1970's.
Cloth embroidered, green back-
ground with white letters and red
border.
Manufactured in Egypt.
Size: 12.0 cm X 2.7 cm.
Item #VIII-3

SHOULDER PATCH/ARCH - SAUDI
ROYAL PARACHUTE CORPS - Worn in
the 1960/70's.
White arabic words on green felt
background.
Manufactured in the Middle East.
Size: 11.5 cm X 3.5 cm.
Item #VIII-4.

SHOULDER PATCH/ARCH - VIP GUARDS
SPECIAL SAFETY UNIT - Worn in the
1970's.
Black arabic words on an orange
cloth background.
Manufactured in the Middle East.
Size: 11.7 cm X 3.7 cm.
Item #VIII-5.

SHOULDER PATCH/ARCH - VIP GUARDS
SPECIAL SAFETY UNIT - Worn in the
1970's.
Black arabic words on an orange
felt background. Black border.
Manufactured in the Middle East.
Size: 10.5 cm X 2.6 cm.
Item #VIII-6.

SHOULDER PATCH/ARCH - SPECIAL
SECURITY FORCES - Worn in the
1970's.
Brown arabic words on an orange
felt background with brown border
Manufactured in the Middle East.
Size: 11.4 cm X 3.3 cm.
Item #VIII-7.

SHOULDER PATCH/ARCH - SECURITY
AND SERVICES UNIT - Worn in the
1970's.
Black arabic words, hand stiched
on a yellow felt background.
Manufactured in the Middle East.
Size: 10.5 cm X 3.3 cm.
Item #VIII-8.

SHOULDER PATCH/ARCH – SPECIAL
UNIT FORCES – Worn in the 1970's.
Yellow arabic words embroidered
on a red felt background with
yellow border.
Manufactured in the Middle East.
Size: 9.8 cm X 2.7 cm.
Item #VIII-9.

SHOULDER PATCH/ARCH – JEDDAH
SPECIAL EMERGENCY UNITS – Worn
in the 1970's.
Black arabic words on red felt
background. Hand stiched.
Manufactured in the Middle East.
Size: 10.8 cm X 3.5 cm.
Item #VIII-10.

SHOULDER PATCH/ARCH - HEJAZ
SECURITY FORCES - Worn in the
1970's.
Yellow arabic words on green
background with red border.
Manufactured in the Middle East.
Size: 10.3 cm X 3.7 cm.
Item #VIII-11.

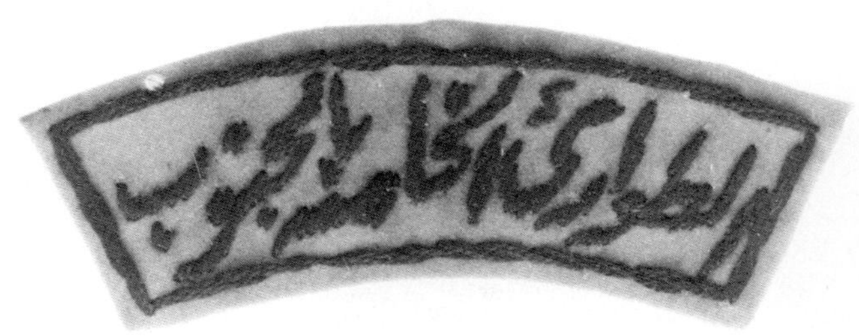

SHOULDER PATCH/ARCH - EMERGENCY
FOR THE SOUTH(YEMEN BORDER) -
Worn in the 1970's.
Black arabic writing on red felt
background with black border.
Manufactured in the Middle East.
Size: 10.8 cm X 3.4 cm.
Item #VIII-12.

SHOULDER PATCH/ARCH - RIYADH
(MIDDLE AREA) SPECIAL EMERGENCY
UNITS - Worn in the 1970's.
Black arabic writing on red felt
background with black border.
Manufactured in the Middle East.
Size: 10.9 cm X 3.5 cm.
Item #VIII-13.

SLEEVE PATCH - SAUDI ARABIAN
COMMAND AND STAFF COLLEGE - Worn
in the 1960/1970's.
Green, gold, black, buff, silver,
brown, blue, white, and red felt
background. Worn in middle of
sleeve. Manufactured in Egypt.
Size: 7.8 cm X 10 cm.Item#VIII-14.

SLEEVE PATCH - SAUDI ARABIAN
COMMAND AND STAFF COLLEGE - Worn
in the 1980's. Cloth embroidered.
Multi colored with rose colored
background. Motto of school:Plan-
ning-implementation-supervision.
Manufactured in Pakistan.
Size: 11.0 cm diameter.Item #15.

SLEEVE PATCH-SAUDI ARABIAN
COMMAND AND STAFF COLLEGE-Worn
in the 1980's. Bullion embroid-
ered. Gold & Silver bullion.
School founded in 1968. Manuf.
in Pakistan.
Size: 11.0 cm diameter.
Item #VIII-16.

SLEEVE PATCH - KING ABDUL-AZIZ
MILITARY ACADEMY - Worn in the
1970/80's. Colors are gold, red,
green, black and white on red
satin background. Arabic reads:
Make ready every possible force
for them. Manuf. in Europe.
Size: 6.5 cm X 8.5 cm.Item #17.

SHOULDER PATCH/ARCH - SAUDI ARAB-
IAN AIR DEFENSE SCHOOL - Worn in
the 1970's.
White arabic writing on green
background. White border.
Manufactured in the Middle East.
Size: 11.7 cm X 3.5 cm.
Item #VIII-18.

SLEEVE PATCH - SAUDI ARABIAN ARMY
AIR DEFENSE ARTILLERY - worn in
the early 1970's.
Yellow missile & cannon on red
felt background.
Manufactured in the Middle East.
Size: 7.2 cm diameter.
Item #VIII-19.

SLEEVE PATCH - SAUDI ARABIAN ARMY
AIR DEFENSE ARTILLERY - worn in
the 1970's and 1980's.
Yellow & white missile and cannon
on red felt background. Merrowed
edge. Manufactured in Taiwan.
Size: 7.2 cm diameter.
Item #VIII-20.

SCHOOL LOGO - SAUDI ARABIAN ARMY
AIR DEFENSE SCHOOL LOGO - Used
in 1978 to 1980's.
Only black & white illustration
available.
Designed in Saudi Arabia.
Size: 5.7 cm X 4.7 cm.
Item #VIII-21.

POCKET PATCH - INSTRUCTOR -SAUDI
ARABIAN ARMY FIELD ARTILLERY
SCHOOL - Worn in the 1970's.
Gold bullion and red thread on
blue twill background.
Manufactured in Pakistan.
Size: 6.5 cm diameter.
Item #VIII-22.

POCKET PATCH –INSTRUCTOR –SAUDI
ARABIAN ARMY FIELD ARTILLERY
SCHOOL – Worn in the 1970's.
Yellow arabic words on green back-
ground. Triangle shape.
Manufactured in the Middle East.
Size: 4.9 cm X 6.7 cm.
Item #VIII-23.

SHOULDER PATCH/ARCH – SAUDI ARAB-
IAN ARMY MEDICAL SERVICE SCHOOL–
Worn in the 1970's.
Yellow arabic words on green back-
ground with white border.
Manufactured in the Middle East.
Size: 11.0 cm X 4.0 cm.
Item #VIII-24.

SHOULDER PATCH/ARCH - SAUDI ARAB-
IAN ARMY MILITARY CLERKS SCHOOL-
Worn in the 1970's.
White arabic words on green back-
ground with white border.
Manufactured in the Middle East.
Size: 11.5 cm X 3.2 cm.
Item #VIII-25.

SHOULDER PATCH/ARCH - SAUDI ARAB-
IAN ARMY SIGNAL CORPS SCHOOL -
Worn in the 1970's.
White arabic words on green back-
ground with white border.
Manufactured in the Middle East.
Size: 11.8 cm X 3.5 cm.
Item #VIII-26.

SHOULDER PATCH/ARCH-ROYAL ARMY
SIGNAL CORPS SCHOOL - Worn in the
1960's
White arabic words on a green back-
ground with white border.
Manufactured in the Middle East.
Size: 12.0 cm X 3.6 cm.
Item #VIII-27.

SHOULDER PATCH/ARCH - SAUDI ARAB-
IAN ARMY SIGNAL CORPS - Worn in
the 1970's.
White arabic words on green back-
ground with white border.
Size: 10.5 cm X 3.6 cm.
Item #VIII-28.

COMMANDO ARCH- SAUDI ARABIA -Worn
in the 1970's.
Gold arabic writing(Al-Seagah) on
black enameled background with
gold border. Pin clip fastener.
Manufactured in Egypt.
Size: 56.8 cm X 2.4 cm.
Item #VIII-29 & II-74.

COMMANDO ARCH-SAUDI ARABIA-Worn in
the 1970's. Copper colored arabic
writing on dull black enameled
background with copper inlaid border. Pin clip fastener.
Manufactured in Egypt for Saudi.
Size: 6.8 cm X 2.4 cm.
Item #VIII-30 & #II-75.

COMMANDO SLEEVE TAB-SAUDI ARABIA-
Worn in the 1960's. Yellow arabic
writing(Al-Seagah) on black cloth.
Manufactured in Saudi Arabia.
Sizes: 6.2cm X 2.4 cm & 7.6cm X
3.4 cm.
Item #VIII-31 & 32 and II-72 & 73.

AIRBORNE/PARACHUTIST ARCH- SAUDI
ARABIA - Worn in the 1970's.
Gold arabic writing(Al-Medallat)
on Red enameled background with
gold border. Pin clip fastener.
Manufactured in Egypt.
Size: 6.8 cm X 2.4 cm.
Item #VIII-33 and II-70.

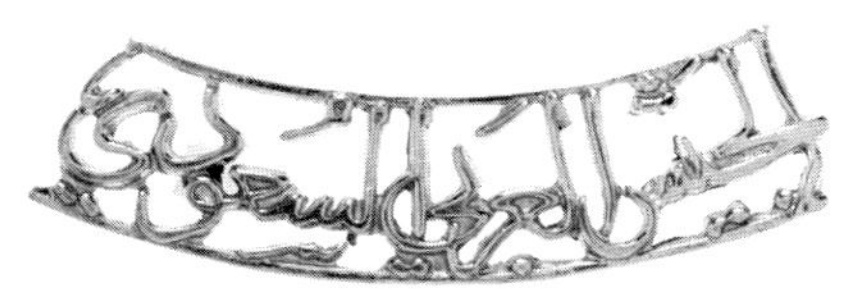

SHOULDER LOOP ARCH - SAUDI ARAB-
IAN ARMY - Worn in the 1980's.
Gold cutout metal with screw post
fastener. Arabic reads: Saudi
Arabian Army. Manufactured in
Korea for Saudi Arabia.
Size: 5.5 cm X 1.3 cm.
Item #VIII-34(Pair)

SHOULDER LOOP ARCH - SAUDI ARAB-
IAN ARMY - Worn in the 1980's.
Gold cutout metal with screw post
fastener. Flat arabic wording.
Manufactured in Egypt for Saudi
Arabia. Larger lettering style.
Size: 6.0 cm X 1.8 cm.
Item #VIII-35(Pair)

Item #VIII-36.

Item #VIII-37.

Item #VIII-38.   151

Item #VIII-39   152

Item #VIII-40

Item #VIII-41

Item #VIII-42

Item #VIII-43   152

Item #VIII-44

Item #VIII-45

Item #VIII-46

Item #VIII-47

Chapter IX illustrates such various uniform items such
s Officer Hats for formal or party wear and service or duty
ats. Additionally Aiquillettes and Ferrules are illustrated.
paulettes/Shoulder Boards for formal or party functions are
hown for officers.

Line drawings are used to illustrate these uniform items.
11 of these items are manufactured in the United States of
merica. These particular designs were adopted in 1978 and
ade available for issue to personnel in 1980.

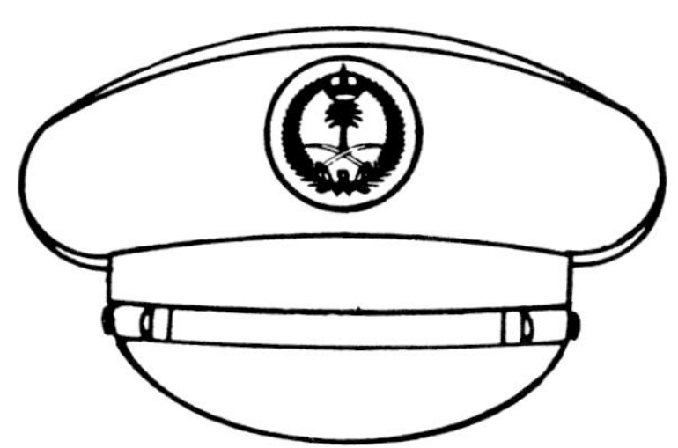

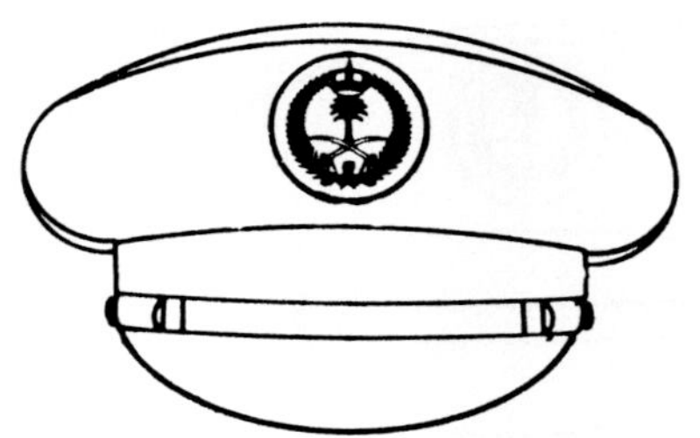

TOP - General Officer Formal(Party)
    Hat. Item #IX-1.
MIDDLE - Field Grade Officer Formal
    (Party) Hat. Item #IX-2.
BOTTOM - Company Grade Officer
    Formal(Party) Hat.Item #IX-3

All hats are black fur felt with
gold ornamentation.

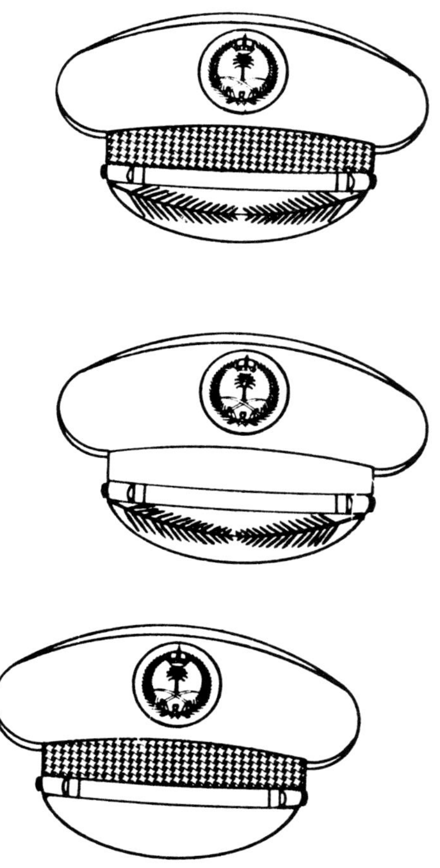

TOP - General Officer Service Hat
    w/ red velvet cap band.
    Item #IX-4.
MIDDLE - Field Grade Officer
    Service Hat. Item #IX-5.
BOTTOM - Company Grade Officer
    Service Hat. Item #IX-6.
All Hats are OG wool elastic.

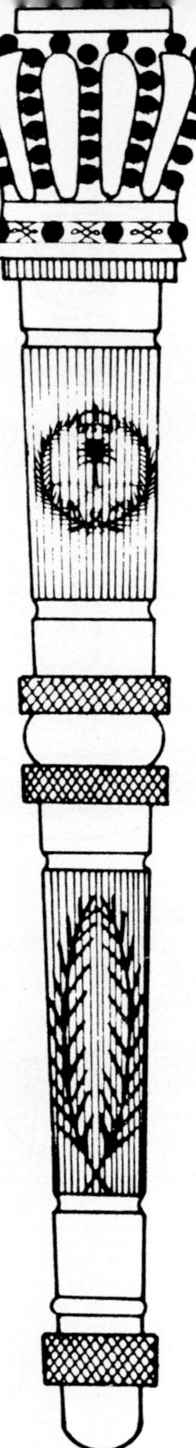

FERRULES - All are gold in color.
AIQUILLETTES:
        Type 1- Gold for Royal Guard,
        Aide, and Military Attache.
        Type 2- Gold for all officers
        Type 3- White for Royal Guard
        Type 4- Red for Military
157   Police. Item #IX-7,8,9. & 10.

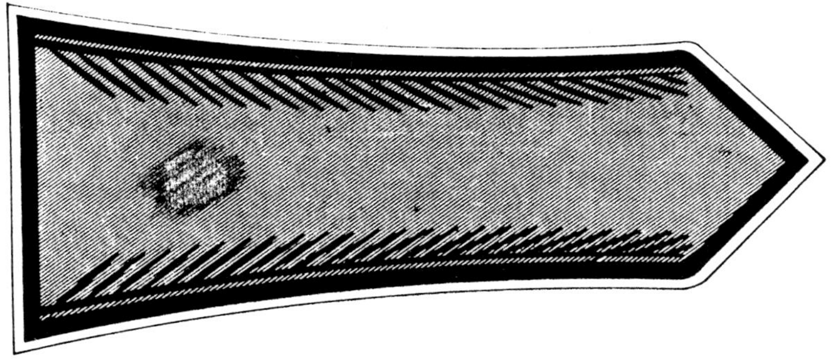

GENERAL OFFICERS – Black Felt
with Gold Embroidery. Item #IX-11.

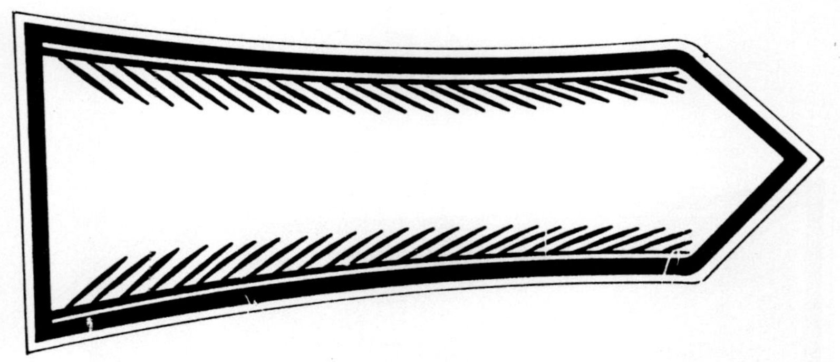

FIELD GRADE OFFICERS - Black Felt
with Gold Line Embroidery.
Item #IX-12.

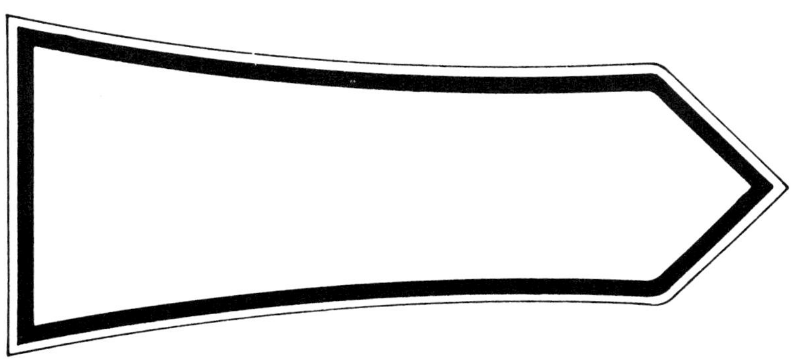

COMPANY GRADE OFFICERS - Gold
Embroidered border. Item #IX-13.

Item #IX-14   Belt Buckle(Tan, OD, or Black
                        webbed belt.)

Item #IX-15

Item #IX-16

Item #IX-17

The Ministry of Defence and Aviation issued a regulation governing the award of Saudi Decorations which includes civilian and military medals, in 1971(1391 A.H.). This regulation was published during the reign of King Faisal Bin Abdul-Aziz Al-Saud.

The specific medals approved were the Medal for Merit, Military Appreciation Medal, Air Falcon Medal, Naval Forces Medal and the King Abdul-Aziz Medal.

The Royal Protocol Department is entrusted with enforcing the medals regulations and the distribution, upon approval(Royal endorsement) of all medals, necklaces, sashes and brevets.

Additionally, service medals are also awarded by the Ministry of Defense and Aviation and have included some of the following:

a. King Abdul Aziz Medal for Syrian and Jordan Service-The ribbon is green and gold.

b. Saudi Arabian Training Medal presented by Syria to Saudi Military personnel - The ribbon is dark blue, light blue and green with a gold palm leaf.

c. The Saudi Arabian 6 October 1973 Medal presented by Syria to Saudi Military personnel - The ribbon is green and yellow with a silver sword.

d. The Saudi Arabian Military Appreciation Medal - The ribbon is red, black and white.

Other ribbons also exist, but are not as well known as those listed above.

All Saudi Decorations, Medals and Ribbons are awarded by authority of the King. With each award of a particular decoration, medal, ribbon, a life time monthly monetary allowance is made to the individual.

Medals/Decorations are also divided into five various classes with a specific annual quota. The classes, in ascending sequence are: 4th class, 3rd class, 2nd class, 1st class and Distinguished Class. Some sash and ribbon awards are divided into five grades: Fourth grade, Third grade, Second grade, First grade and Excellent grade. Some medals are graded with the color of the medal determining the grade, such as Bronze(Third Grade), Silver(Second Grade), and Gold(First Grade).

All medals and decorations are of quality design and materials, regardless of the grade or class. The following pages illustrate the cover of the medals regulation.

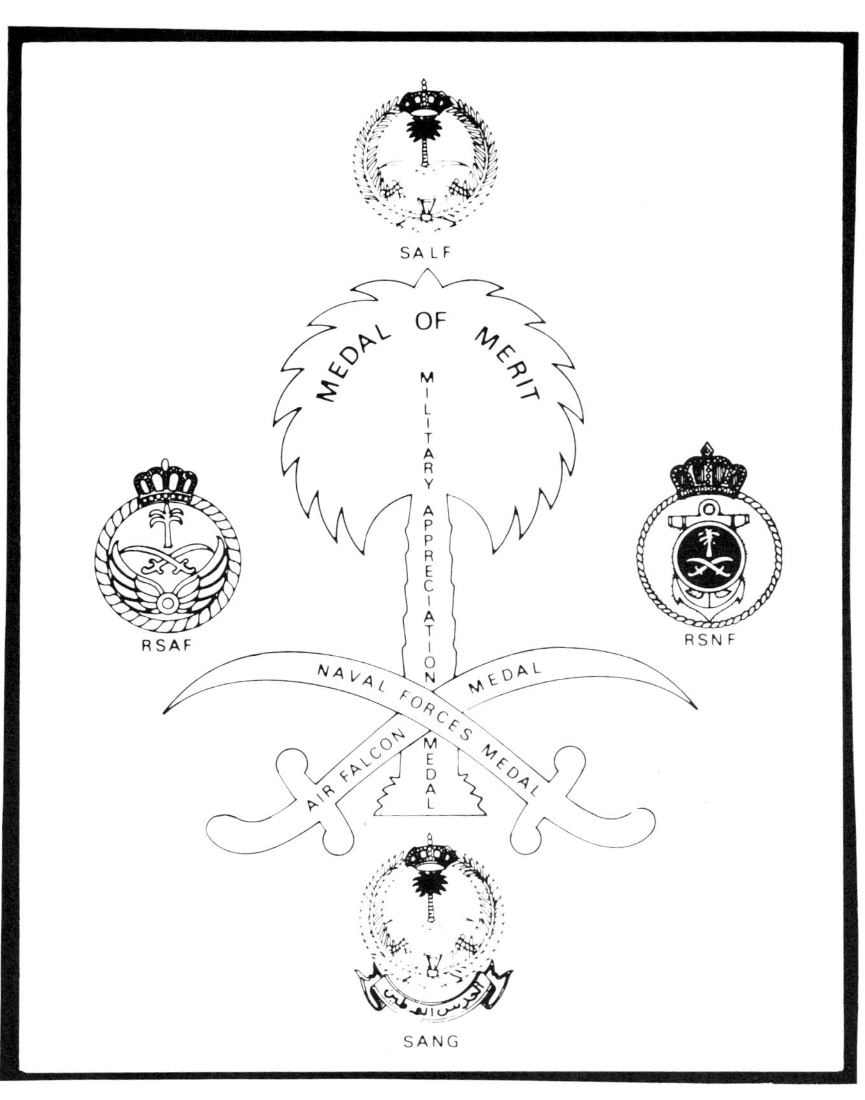

MEDALS AND DECORATIONS REGULATION
Item #X-1.

Item #X-2   Item #X-3   Item #X-4

Item #X-5   Item #X-6   Item #X-7

Item #X-8   Item #X-9   Item #X-10

Item #X-11   Item #X-12

U.S. GOVERNMENT ORGANIZATIONS IN SAUDI ARABIA
CHAPTER XI

The United States of America has five(5) primary governmental operations in the Kingdom of Saudi Arabia. Each operation was established by a Memorandum of Understanding. All of these various operations are fully funded by the Saudi Arabian Government, just as they would pay for the services of any U.S., British, French, Korean, Pakistani, or German company.

The largest operation is the U.S. Corps of Engineers, which is involved in extensive governmental construction projects for the Saudi Arabian Land Forces.

The Saudi Arabian National Guard Modernization Project is operated by the U.S.Army DARCOM, Dept.of Defense, and involves training, construction, equipment procurement and equipment maintenance.

The USREP/JECOR, Joint Economic Commission is a project operated by the U.S.Treasury Department and involves technical assistance to the various Saudi Arabian Governmental Ministries. Personnel from all branches of the U.S. government are assigned to the USREP/JECOR Team.

The U.S. Military Training Mission is a project operated by the Department of Defense, U.S. Security Assistance Center, which is involved in military training assistance to the Army, Navy, and Air Force.

A sub-activity of the Corps of Engineers is the Ordnance Program Division, Saudi Ordnance Corps Program, which is an assistance project to the Saudi Arabian Army Ordnance Corps, Ministry of Defence and Aviation.

The U.S. Embassy is a permanent organization, which is involved in the diplomatic aspects of our official relations with Saudi Arabia. Various nation building projects also come under the jurisdiction of the U.S. Embassy.

Various patches, badges, insignia, and logos have evolved over the years for these primary organizations as well as sub-organizations. The main theme that is depicted is that of mutual and beneficial cooperation between the Government of Saudi Arabia(SAG) and the United States Government(USG).

The following pages show all known insignia/badges plus a few items worn by the French Advisors to Saudi Arabia.

U.S. ARMY CORPS OF ENGINEERS, MIDDLE
EAST DIVISION SHOULDER PATCH.
Red & White patch with white merrowed
edge. Manufactured in the U.S.A.
Worn on Green Uniform by U.S. military
personnel assigned to USAEDME & (Rear).
Size-7.6cm X 7.9cm. Item #XI —1(colored)
                         Item #XI —2(subdued)

U.S. ARMY CORPS OF ENGINEERS, MIDDLE
EAST DIVISION & DISTRICTS POCKET BADGE.
Gold metal, two piece Saudi Hat Badge
affixed to brown leather holder. Worn
attached to tan & green shirt pocket
button. Worn by U.S. military personnel.
Size-4.2cm diameter. Item #XI —3(badge)
                         Item #XI —3a(holder

U.S. CORPS OF ENGINEERS, KINGDOM OF
SAUDI ARABIA POCKET PATCH. Tan patch
with red, black and green letters.
Manufactured in Taiwan. Worn beginning
in 1979 on windbreakers by U.S. military
personnel. Size-7.2-7.7cm X 9.0-9.3cm.
Item #XI -4; XI -5; XI -6.

U.S. CORPS OF ENGINEERS, SAUDI ARABIA
ENGINEER LOGISTICS COMMAND, AVIATION
DETACHMENT, RIYADH, POCKET PATCH-Small.
Manufactured in the Phillipines. Limited
number made pending re-supply of U.S.
made patches. Worn on fatiques & flight
suits by U.S. military aviators.
Size-9.2cm diameter.Item #XI -7,8, & 9.

U.S. CORPS OF ENGINEERS, SAUDI ARABIA,
ENGINEER LOGISTICS COMMAND, AVIATION
DETACHMENT, RIYADH-POCKET PATCH-Large.
Manufactured in the Phillipines. Limited
number made pending re-supply of U.S.
made patches. Worn on fatiques & flight
suits by U.S. military aviators.
Size-12.7cm diameter.Item #XI -10 & 11.

U.S. CORPS OF ENGINEERS, SAUDI ARABIA,
ENGINEER LOGISTICS COMMAND, AVIATION
DETACHMENT, RIYADH-POCKET PATCH-Large.
Manufactured in the U.S.A. Worn from
1975 todate by all U.S. military &
civilian contract aviators on flight
suits. Size-12.7cm diameter.
Item #XI -12.

U.S. ARMY ENGINEER DISTRICT, SAUDI
ARABIA - POCKET PATCH.
Manufactured in the Phillipines. Worn
by engineer personnel during the period
1965 to 1975. Worn on windbreakers.
Size-11.4cm diameter. Item #XI -13.

U.S. ARMY ENGINEER DISTRICT, RIYADH-
KINGDOM OF SAUDI ARABIA - POCKET PATCH.
Manufactured in the Phillipines. Worn
by District Engineer personnel primarily
on civilian jackets during the period
1978 to date. Size-11.4 cm diameter.
Item #XI -14.

U.S. MILITARY TRAINING MISSION, SAUDI
ARABIA - POCKET PATCH - Small.
Manufactured in Taiwan. Worn by U.S.
military advisors prior to 1976.
Size-6.0-6.3cm diameter.
Item #XI -15 & XI -16.

U.S. MILITARY TRAINING MISSION, SAUDI
ARABIA - POCKET PATCH - Large.
Manufactured in the Phillipines. Two
types - white background & tan background. Worn on jackets from 1980 to
date. Size-11.0-11.4cm diameter.
Item #XI -17 & XI -18.

U.S. MILITARY TRAINING MISSION, SAUDI
ARABIA - POCKET BADGE & HOLDER.
Manufactured in the U.S.A. by V-21.
Worn by advisory personnel from 1978
to date. Worn by all services. Size-
4.1cm diameter. Item #XI -19(Badge)
                    #XI -19a(Holder)

U.S. MILITARY TRAINING MISSION, SAUDI
ARABIA - POCKET PATCH- Small.
Manufactured in Pakistan. Royal Saudi
Navy design incorporated into patch.
Worn on jackets of U.S. Navy personnel
assigned to USMTM. Worn from 1980 to
date. Size-5cm diameter.
Item #XI -20.

OFFICE OF THE PROJECT MANAGER, SAUDI
ARABIAN NATIONAL GUARD MODERNIZATION-
POCKET PATCH-Large.
Manufactured in Phillipines-small &
in Taiwan-large.Worn on jackets from
1980 todate by military & civilians.
Size-9.0-10.0cm diameter. DARCOM project
Item #XI -21 & XI -22.

OFFICE OF THE PROJECT MANAGER, SAUDI
ARABIAN NATIONAL GUARD MODERNIZATION-
POCKET BADGE & HOLDER.
Gold single piece Saudi National Guard
Agau Badge attached to leather holder.
Worn by U.S. military advisors on shirt
pocket flap button, from 1978 to date.
Size-3.8cm X 5cm. Item #XI -23(Badge)
                        #XI -23a(Holder)

SAUDI ARABIAN ARMY ORDNANCE CORPS,SOCP,
U.S. CORPS OF ENGINEERS-POCKET PATCH.
Manufactured in the Phillipines. Worn
in late 1970's on jackets of advisors.
Size-7.5-10.6cm X 10.2-12.4cm.
Item #XI -24 & XI -25.

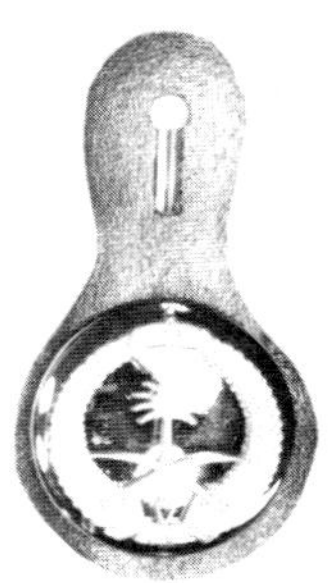

SAAOC, TABUK NOVELTY JACKET PATCH — 1979
Manufactured in Pakistan with bullion crossed
swords. Designed by former OPD Advisor to
SAAOC, Tabuk Area.
Size: 10.7 cm diameter. Item #XI-26.
SAAOC/OPD ADVISOR POCKET BADGE — 1979 & 1980's
Item #XI-27. Size: Same as Item #XI-3 & 3a.
     #XI-27a(Holder)

U.S. ARMY TROOP SUPPORT AGENCY, U.S.
ARMY COMMISSARY STORES-POCKET PATCH.
Manufactured in the U.S.A. Worn in
1979 to date by U.S. military personnel
in Dhahran, Riyadh & Jeddah commissaries.
Size-9.2cm X 11.2cm. Item #XI -28.

USREP/JECOR- JOINT ECONOMIC COMMISSION-
POCKET PATCH.
U.S. Treasury Department Project. Worn
by civilians on jackets since 1980.
Cloth & Bullion variations-made in
Pakistan. Size-11.1cm diameter.
Item #XI -29 & XI -30.

MISSION MILITAIRE FRANCAISE EN ARABIE
SAOUDITE - SHOULDER PATCH. Worn by
French Military Mission Personnel.
Size-7.4cm X 10cm. Item #XI -31.
COFRAS-COMPAIGNIE FRANCAISE ASSISTANCE
SPECIALISEE-POCKET BADGE. Worn by French
advisors to Saudi Armor Corps & Ord.Corp
Size-3.5cm X 4.5cm. Item #XI -32.

U.S. CORPS OF ENGINEERS, AL BATIN
DISTRICT, SAUDI ARABIA - POCKET PATCH
Manufactured in the U.S.A. Worn by
U.S. Military & Civilians on jackets
& caps, since 1980.
Size-10.0cm X 7.0cm. Item #XI -33.

UNITED STATES ARMY SECURITY ASSISTANCE
CENTER-USASAC. Logistic Activity
responsible for support to friendly
nations.
Size- 5½cm X 6½cm. Item #XI -34.

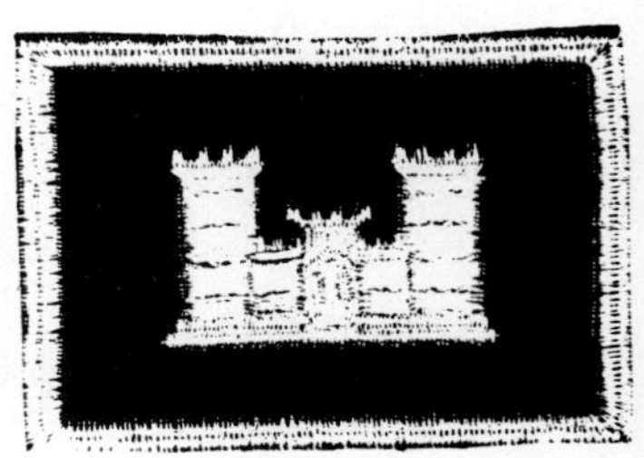

U.S. ARMY CORPS OF ENGINEERS PATCHES -
The above patches were worn prior to 1980
by civilian engineers and technicians
assigned to the U.S. Army Corps of Engineers.
Item #XI -36 & #XI -37.

Item #XI-38

Item #XI-39

UNITED STATES EUROPEAN COMMAND-USECOM.
Controling Headquarters for all Military
Training Missions, including USMTM,SA.
 Size-8cm X 8cm.   Item #XI -35.

Item #XI-40

Item #XI-41

Item #XI-42

Item #XI-43

Item #XI-44

Item #XI-45

Item #XI-46

Item #XI-47

Item #XI-48

BIBLIOGRAPHY/REFERENCES
CHAPTER XII

1. <u>Area Handbook for Saudi Arabia</u> - 1971, Second Edition(DA Pam 550-51) U.S. Govt. Printing Office, Library of Congress Catalog Number 67-5743, compiled by Foreign Area Studies, American University, 5010 Wisconsin Ave., N.W. Washington, D.C. 20016.

2. <u>Area Handbook for Saudi Arabia</u> - 1977, Third Edition(DA Pam 550-51) U.S. Govt. Printing Office, Library of Congress Catalog Number 76-51268, compiled by Foreign Area Studies, American University, 5010 Wisconsin Ave., N.W., Washington, D.C. 20016.

3. <u>Regulations governing the award of the Saudi Decorations and Civilian and Military Medals Regulation, 1971(1391 A.H.)</u> by the General Staff Headquarters, G1, Military Affairs, Ministry of Defense and Aviation, Kingdom of Saudi Arabia - translated from the original arabic.

4. <u>Parachute Badges and Insignia of the World</u>, 1979, by R.J. Bragg and Roy Turner, published by Blandford Press Ltd., Link House, West Street, Poole, Dorset BH 15 ILL ISBN 0 713708824.

5. <u>A Dictionary of Military Uniforms</u>, 1977, by W. Y. Carman, published by Charles Scribner's Sons, New York, New York, ISBN 0-068-15130-8.

6. <u>The Arab Legion</u>, 1972, by Brig. Peter Young, Osprey Publishing Ltd., P.O. Box 251, 707 Oxford Road, Reading, Berkshire, England.

7. <u>Armies of the Middle East</u>, 1979, by Otto Van Pivka Printed in Great Britain, distributed by Mayflower Books, Inc., New York, New York, ISBN 0-8317-0443-8.

8. <u>Elusive Victory</u>, 1978, by Trevor N. Dupuy, Harper and Row, Publisher, New York, New York, ISBN 0-06-011112-7.

9. <u>Assault from the Sky, A History of Airborne Warfare</u>, 1978, by John Weeks, published by G.P. Putnam's Sons, 200 Madison Avenue, New York, New York

10. <u>Heraldry and Regalia of War</u>, 1973, edited by Bernard Fitzsimons, Phoebus, London, BPC Publishing Ltd., Beekman House, div. of Crown Publishers, Inc New York, New York, ISBN 0-517-130866.

Chapter VII

VII-1	VII-2	VII-3	VII-4	VII-5	VII-6
VII-7	VII-8	VII-9	VII-10	VII-11	VII-12
VII-13	VII-14	VII-15	VII-16	VII-17	VII-18
VII-19	VII-20	VII-21	VII-22	VII-23	VII-24
VII-25	VII-26	VII-27	VII-28	VII-29	VII-30
VII-31	VII-32	VII-33	VII-34	VII-35	VII-36
VII-37	VII-38	VII-39	VII-40	VII-41	VII-42
VII-43	VII-44	VII-45	VII-46	VII-47	VII-48
VII-49	VII-50	VII-51	VII-52	VII-53	VII-54
VII-55	VII-56	VII-57	VII-58	VII-59	VII-60
VII-61	VII-62	VII-63	VII-64	VII-65	VII-66
VII-67	VII-68	VII-69	VII-70	VII-71	VII-72
VII-73	VII-74	VII-75	VII-76	VII-77	VII-78
VII-79	VII-80	VII-81	VII-82	VII-83	VII-84
VII-85	VII-86	VII-87	VII-88	VII-89	VII-90

Chapter VIII

VIII-1	VIII-2	VIII-3	VIII-4	VIII-5	VIII-6
VIII-7	VIII-8	VIII-9	VIII-10	VIII-11	VIII-12
VIII-13	VIII-14	VIII-15	VIII-16	VIII-17	VIII-18
VIII-19	VIII-20	VIII-21	VIII-22	VIII-23	VIII-24
VIII-25	VIII-26	VIII-27	VIII-28	VIII-29	VIII-30
VIII-31	VIII-32	VIII-33	VIII-34	VIII-35	VIII-36
VIII-37	VIII-38	VIII-39	VIII-40	VIII-41	VIII-42
VIII-43	VIII-44	VIII-45	VIII-46	VIII-47	VIII-48

Chapter IX

IX-1	IX-2	IX-3	IX-4	IX-5	IX-6
IX-7	IX-8	IX-9	IX-10	IX-11	IX-12
IX-13	IX-14	IX-15	IX-16	IX-17	IX-18

Chapter X

X-1	X-2	X-3	X-4	X-5	X-6
X-7	X-8	X-9	X-10	X-11	X-12

Chapter XI

XI-1	XI-2	XI-3	XI-4	XI-5	XI-6
XI-7	XI-8	XI-9	XI-10	XI-11	XI-12
XI-13	XI-14	XI-15	XI-16	XI-17	XI-18
XI-19	XI-20	XI-21	XI-22	XI-23	XI-24
XI-25	XI-26	XI-27	XI-28	XI-29	XI-30
XI-31	XI-32	XI-33	XI-34	XI-35	XI-36
XI-37	XI-38	XI-39	XI-40	XI-41	XI-42
XI-43	XI-44	XI-45	XI-46	XI-47	XI-48

Chapter XII - No illustrations

Chapter XIII-No illustrations

Chapter XIV -No illustrations

Chapter XV -No illustrations

CHAPTER XIV
COLLECTORS NOTES

184

COLLECTORS NOTES